PRAY
HARD

Books by Kevin Johnson

Early Teen Devotionals

Can I Be a Christian Without Being Weird?
Could Someone Wake Me Up Before I Drool on the Desk?
Does Anybody Know What Planet My Parents Are From?
So Who Says I Have to Act My Age?
Was That a Balloon or Did Your Head Just Pop?
Who Should I Listen To?
Why Can't My Life Be a Summer Vacation?
Why Is God Looking for Friends?

Early Teen Discipleship

Get God: Make Friends With the King of the Universe
Wise Up: Stand Clear of the Unsmartness of Sin
Cross Train: Blast Through the Bible From Front to Back
Pray Hard: Talk to God With Total Confidence
See Jesus: Peer Into the Life and Mind of Your Master
Stick Tight: Glue Yourself to Godly Friends
Get Smart: Unscramble Mind-Boggling Questions of Your Faith
Bust Loose: Become the Wild New Person You Are in Jesus

Books for Youth

Catch the Wave!
Find Your Fit[1]
God's Will, God's Best[2]
Jesus Among Other Gods: Youth Edition[3]
Look Who's Toast Now!
What's With the Dudes at the Door?[4]
What's With the Mutant in the Microscope?[4]
What Do Ya Know?
Where Ya Gonna Go?

To find out more about Kevin Johnson's books or speaking availability
visit his Web site: www.thewave.org

[1]with Jane Kise   [2]with Josh McDowell   [3]with Ravi Zacharias   [4]with James White

EARLY TEEN DISCIPLESHIP

Talk to God With Total Confidence

PRAY HARD

Kevin Johnson

BETHANYHOUSE
MINNEAPOLIS, MINNESOTA

Published by Bethany House Publishers
A Ministry of Bethany Fellowship International
11400 Hampshire Avenue South
Bloomington, Minnesota 55438
www.bethanyhouse.com

Printed in the United States of America by
Bethany Press International, Bloomington, Minnesota 55438

Library of Congress Cataloging-in-Publication Data

Johnson, Kevin (Kevin Walter)
    Pray hard : talk to God with total confidence / by Kevin Johnson.
       p. cm. — (Early teen discipleship)
    ISBN 1–55661–639–2 (pbk.)
    1. Prayer—Christianity—Juvenile literature. 2. Christian teenagers—
Religious life—Juvenile literature. 3. Bible—Textbooks. [1. Prayer books
and devotions. 2. Christian life.] I. Title.
    BS212 .J64 2001
    248.8′2—dc21

                                                                    00–012015

To Gail, Daryl, and Jessica

You show us what love looks like.

KEVIN JOHNSON is the bestselling author or co-author of more than twenty books for youth, including *Can I Be a Christian Without Being Weird?* and *Catch the Wave!* A full-time author and speaker, he served as senior editor for adult nonfiction at Bethany House Publishers and pastored a group of more than four hundred sixth through ninth graders at Elmbrook Church in metro Milwaukee. While his training includes an M.Div. from Fuller Theological Seminary and a B.A. in English and Print Journalism from the University of Wisconsin–River Falls, his current interests include cycling, guitar, and shortwave radio. Kevin and his wife, Lyn, live in Minnesota with their three children—Nate, Karin, and Elise.

Contents

Part 3: Parts of Prayer

Part 4: Biggie Things to Pray For

Part 5: Grabbing Hold of God

How to Use This Book

Welcome to *Pray Hard*. This book is part of the EARLY TEEN DISCIPLE-
SHIP series, better remembered by its clever initials, ETD. I wrote
ETD as a follow-up to my series of bestselling devotionals—books
like *Can I Be a Christian Without Being Weird?* and *Could Someone Wake Me
Up Before I Drool on the Desk?* ETD has one aim: to help you take your
next step in becoming wildly devoted to Jesus. If you're ready to
work on a vital, heart-to-heart, sold-out relationship with God, this
is your series.

The goal of *Pray Hard* is to help you talk to God with *total* confidence. It'll show you *why* you can talk to him and *what* to say—and
why you'd *want* to pray. *Pray Hard* prods you toward that goal
through twenty-five Bible studies designed to make you think—
okay, without *totally* breaking your brain. It will help you

- dig into Scripture on your own
- feed on insights that you might not otherwise find
- hit the heart issues that push you away from God or pull you
  closer to him.

You can pick your own pace—anything from a study a day to a
study a week. But here's what you'll find in each study:

- Your first stop is BRAIN DRAIN—your spot at the beginning of
  each lesson to spout what you think.
- Then there's FLASHBACK—a bit of background so you better
  understand what's coming up.
- Don't skip over the BIBLE CHUNK—a hand-picked Bible passage
  to read.
- You get STUFF TO KNOW—questions to help you dig into what
  a passage means.
- There's INSIGHT—facts about the passage you might not figure
  out on your own.
- DA'SCOOP—definitions of weird words.
- And SIDELIGHT—other Bible verses that let you see the topic
  from a different angle.

The other big questions are, well . . .

- BIG QUESTIONS—your chance to apply what you have learned to your life.
- Each study wraps up with a DEEP THOT—a thought to chew on.

  But that's not the end.

- There's STICKY STUFF—a Bible verse to jam into your brain juice.
- PRAY ABOUT IT—a one-or-two-liner to use to talk to God. No big fluffy prayers here. Just something to get you going. And it's okay if that's all you say.
- And DIG ON—another Bible passage to unearth if you want more.

And one more thing: There are cards in the back of the book for all the verses in STICKY STUFF, with a few bonus cards thrown in—since we'd already killed the tree.

If you've got a pencil and know how to use it, you're all set.

EXCEPT FOR ONE THING You can study *Pray Hard* on your own. But you can also work through this book with a friend or in a group. After every five studies there's a page called "Talk About It." Nope—you don't have to cover every question on the page. There are too many to answer, so pick the ones that matter most to you.

Whenever you do an ETD study with one friend or a bunch, keep in mind three goals—and three big questions to help you remember those goals. And nope—you don't have to actually ask those questions each time, because that would feel canned. But each time you meet you want to

- EMPATHIZE: *What's gone on since the last time you got together?* To "empathize" means to put yourself in someone else's shoes. Galatians 6:2 tells us to "carry each other's burdens" (NIV), or to "share each other's troubles and problems" (NLT). Whether you call them "highs and lows," "wows and pows," "uppers and downers," or "wins and wedgies," take time to celebrate and support each other by chatting through life's important happenings and offering simple, to-the-point prayers.
- ENCOURAGE: *Where are you at with Jesus?* Hebrews 3:13 says to "encourage one another daily. . . so that none of you may be

hardened by sin's deceitfulness." Religious rules apart from a relationship with God are deadly. So instead be real: Are you growing closer to or wandering away from the Lord you're learning to follow? Is anything tripping you up?

- EQUIP: *What one truth are you going to take away from today that will help you live closer to Jesus?* Second Timothy 3:16–17 promises that "All Scripture is inspired by God and is useful to teach us what is true and to make us realize what is wrong in our lives. It straightens us out and teaches us to do what is right. It is God's way of preparing us in every way, fully equipped for every good thing God wants us to do" (NLT). Don't leave your get-together without one point of truth that will make a difference in your life. It might not be the thought or verse that anyone else picks. But grab at least one truth—and hang on tight by letting it make a difference in your life.

Got it? Not only is *Pray Hard* a study to do on your own, but better yet, it can help you grow your faith with your friends. You can pick a leader—a youth or adult—or take turns picking questions and talking through them as your time allows. Just keep the three big goals in mind.

Now you're ready. You can do it. Grow ahead and turn the page and get started.

PART 1

GETTING GOD'S BEST

1. Talk to the Bush
God wants to talk with you

"Pray?" Megan bunches up her face. "Out loud? Me?" Five other campers and a counselor sharing the dining hall table with Megan all sit with their thumbs up. "Last one with thumbs up has to say grace," says the kid next to her. "You lose."

BRAIN DRAIN Do you sweat when people ask you to pray? How come—or not?

FLASHBACK This Bible Chunk isn't exactly about prayer, though it *is* about talking with God. Way back toward the beginning of the Bible, God had decided to free his people from slavery in Egypt—a plotline you maybe know from the Bible book of Exodus or the oldie movie *The Ten Commandments*. First, though, God needed to chat with a man named Moses. Sometimes when you pray you might wonder if you're babbling words into the air. Moses had it easy. He got to talk to a bush.

BIBLE CHUNK Read Exodus 3:1–14

(1) Now Moses was tending the flock of Jethro his father-in-law, the priest of Midian, and he led the flock to the far side of the desert and came to Horeb, the mountain of God. (2) There the angel of the Lord appeared to him in flames of fire from within a bush. Moses saw that though the bush was on fire it did not burn up. (3) So Moses thought, "I will go over and see this strange sight—why the bush does not burn up."

(4) When the Lord saw that he had gone over to look, God called to him from within the bush, "Moses! Moses!"

And Moses said, "Here I am."

(5) "Do not come any closer," God said. "Take off your sandals, for the place where you are standing is holy ground." (6) Then he said, "I am the God of your father, the God of Abraham, the God of Isaac and the God of Jacob." At this, Moses hid his face, because he was afraid to look at God.

(7) The Lord said, "I have indeed seen the misery of my people in Egypt. I have heard them crying out because of their slave drivers, and I am concerned about their suffering. (8) So I have come down to rescue them from the hand of the Egyptians and to bring them up out of that land into a good and spacious land, a land flowing with milk and honey—the home of the Canaanites, Hittites, Amorites, Perizzites, Hivites and Jebusites. (9) And now the cry of the Israelites has reached me, and I have seen the way the Egyptians are oppressing them. (10) So now, go. I am sending you to Pharaoh to bring my people the Israelites out of Egypt."

(11) But Moses said to God, "Who am I, that I should go to Pharaoh and bring the Israelites out of Egypt?"

(12) And God said, "I will be with you. And this will be the sign to you that it is I who have sent you: When you have brought the people out of Egypt, you will worship God on this mountain."

(13) Moses said to God, "Suppose I go to the Israelites and say to them, 'The God of your fathers has sent me to you,' and they ask me, 'What is his name?' Then what shall I tell them?"

(14) God said to Moses, "I am who I am. This is what you are to say to the Israelites: 'I am has sent me to you.' "

STUFF TO KNOW What's Moses doing at the start of this Bible Chunk? Do you suppose he expected to run into God (verse 1)?

As Moses is moseying with his sheep, what does he see (verses 2–3)?

INSIGHT Skeptics who dislike miracles think Moses must have seen sun glinting off red leaves. But Moses had tended sheep in the scrubland for forty years and knew a weird sight when he saw one—like a bush that burned without turning to ash.

Okay, so Moses doesn't exactly talk to a bush. He talks to God. What does God tell Moses to do (verse 5)? How does Moses react (verse 6)?

*SIDELIGHT God is separate. Different. Pure. He's what the Bible calls "holy." As the Creator and Owner of the universe, he deserves utter respect. There's something ultra-special about his presence, and Moses knew better than to tromp too close. Getting near to God is the kind of awe-striking experience that causes people to ask, "Who can stand in the presence of the Lord, this holy God?" (1 Samuel 6:20).

God had incredible stuff he wanted to give his people—like freedom from slavery and a homeland where they could live close to him. Moses argued that he wasn't qualified to deal with God or do his work. One last question: What does God tell Moses to call him?

INSIGHT Everybody already knew God's name. The voice Moses heard was "the God of Abraham, Isaac, and Jacob." But God's people were wondering if he had left them to rot in slavery. "I AM WHO I AM" doesn't just say that God is the being who's been around forever. It means "I am the God who is with you."

BIG QUESTIONS Why do you suppose Moses was scared to be face-to-face with God?

Do you figure it was easy for Moses to talk with God speaking from "within the bush"? Why or why not?

When God says "Jump!" Moses hardly says "How high?" Does Moses sound like he's mouthing off? What do you think of the way he talks to God?

DEEP THOT Cool news: God wants to talk with you. But it can be hard knowing what to say to an all-powerful God you can't see. The goal of *Pray Hard* is for you to learn both *how* and *why* you can talk to God with total confidence.

STICKY STUFF Put Exodus 3:14 in your brain to remind yourself how God introduced himself. There's a card in the back of *Pray Hard* to help your memory.

PRAY ABOUT IT *God, help me believe that you want to talk with me.*

DIG ON Read Psalm 24:1–4 for an Old Testament perspective on daring to enter the presence of God.

②. Better Than a Topped-Off Coffin
God wants to give you good gifts

✳When ancient Egyptians buried a dead body they packed the tomb with all the treasure and trinkets a person would need after death—as if a mummy would need much. God doesn't plan to fill your coffin and fly you to the land of the dead. He wants to set you up with everything you need to survive and thrive in *life*. The catch? He won't load you up if you don't want his help.

BRAIN DRAIN Do you think God is glad to give to you— or is he a grouch?

✳**FLASHBACK** In the two Bible chapters before this chunk, Jesus covers a load of the basics of the Christian faith. In his "Sermon on the Mount" Jesus tells his followers how they'll flip the world upside down. He challenges them to love their enemies. He teaches them that God cares about everything they need in life— like food and clothes. And after Jesus informs them of all that, he tells them to go knocking at the one source who could load them up right. They should go to the God who will "meet all [their] needs according to his glorious riches in Christ Jesus" (Philippians 4:19).

✳**BIBLE CHUNK** Read Matthew 7:7–11

(7) "Ask and it will be given to you; seek and you will find; knock and the door will be opened to you. (8) For everyone who asks receives; he

who seeks finds; and to him who knocks, the door will be opened.

(9) "Which of you, if his son asks for bread, will give him a stone? (10) Or if he asks for a fish, will give him a snake? (11) If you, then, though you are evil, know how to give good gifts to your children, how much more will your Father in heaven give good gifts to those who ask him!"

STUFF TO KNOW Jesus just spent what amounts to two long Bible chapters detailing what it looks like to be his follower. What's the next thing he says (verse 7)?

Those three verbs—*ask, seek,* and *knock*—are in a tense that means "do it and keep doing it" (verses 7–8). What will happen if you . . .

- Ask?

- Seek?

- Knock?

How do human parents react when their kids present their needs to them (verses 9–10)?

Is that reaction like God's? How (verse 11)?

INSIGHT Some human beings are capable of chopping others up and serving them in soup—or sewing lampshades out of skin. Yet most know how to wisely provide for their kids. They wouldn't think of giving a child a hunk of rock masquerading as bread or a hunk of anything different and deadly.

So what does all this say about what kind of gifts God wants to give us (verse 11)?

*SIDELIGHT The kind of gifts God plans for you shout a big mouthful about your relationship with him. When you pray, you're not begging from some stranger. You're talking to your Father. And what he has for you is great, as flawless as his love for you. James 1:17 says, "Every good and perfect gift is from above, coming down from the Father of the heavenly lights, who does not change like shifting shadows."

BIG QUESTIONS Before this Bible Chunk Jesus had said that God knows exactly what you need even before a request leaves your lips (Matthew 6:8). So why bother to pray?

Here's a hint: What would you learn about getting along with God through prayer?

*INSIGHT Some starters: Prayer teaches you to ask respectfully, to seek by saying what you mean and meaning what you say, to knock persistently—and to expect great things from God.

And what will you discover about God when you take your needs to him?

SIDELIGHT You're not praying to a grouchy God. Jesus told a wild story about a guy who goes to a friend's house in the middle of the night to borrow bread. "Can't you tell the doors are locked? We're all in bed!" the bugged friend hollers back. Yet he gave his friend what he needed. If humans can manage to open their doors in the middle of the night, just think how much more eager God is to give (Luke 11:5–8).

DEEP THOT You don't have to bully or beg God to answer your prayers. He doesn't play tricks. He's even smart enough to give you only good gifts.

STICKY STUFF Hang on to Matthew 7:7. It's one of the biggest promises in the Bible.

PRAY ABOUT IT *God, help me trust that you want to give me great gifts.*

DIG ON Take a gander at God's gargantuan promise in Matthew 21:22.

③ Attitude Check
One reason God says no to prayers

"Give it to me!" you screech as you rip the remote control away from your little brother. He screeches back. Then Dad pops into the room. He surveys the situation. Both sides are being bratlike. You've got three seconds to guess the automatic parental response. *Tick . . . tick . . . tick.* You got it: "If you can't watch TV without fighting, then you can't watch at all."

BRAIN DRAIN When have you fought to get something you really wanted—something you later decided was sort of stupid?

*FLASHBACK God has a heap of good gifts. But if God is so eager to share, then why don't you get whatever you ask for? Big news: Just because you plop a desire before God doesn't mean that his saying yes! would be a hot idea. Sometimes you want a thing he doesn't stock in his storehouse—he's got nothing evil, not one thing that's hurtful. Or you're asking for something he won't do—like forcing a friend's divorcing parents back together against their wills. You might be hankering for the right thing—but at the wrong time. Later in *Pray Hard* you'll look at instances where it's truly hard to know why God says no to your request. But sometimes his reason is simple: Your attitude needs rearranging.

BIBLE CHUNK Read James 4:1–10

(1) What causes fights and quarrels among you? Don't they come from your desires that battle within you? (2) You want something but don't get

it. You kill and covet, but you cannot have what you want. You quarrel and fight. You do not have, because you do not ask God. (3) When you ask, you do not receive, because you ask with wrong motives, that you may spend what you get on your pleasures.

(4) You adulterous people, don't you know that friendship with the world is hatred toward God? Anyone who chooses to be a friend of the world becomes an enemy of God. (5) Or do you think Scripture says without reason that the spirit he caused to live in us envies intensely? (6) But he gives us more grace. That is why Scripture says:

"God opposes the proud
but gives grace to the humble."

(7) Submit yourselves, then, to God. Resist the devil, and he will flee from you. (8) Come near to God and he will come near to you. Wash your hands, you sinners, and purify your hearts, you double-minded. (9) Grieve, mourn and wail. Change your laughter to mourning and your joy to gloom. (10) Humble yourselves before the Lord, and he will lift you up.

STUFF TO KNOW Answer the question James asks

in verse 1: What causes the fights between people (verses 2–3)?

Why don't people have what they want (verse 2)?

So when people do go to God, why don't they get what they're looking for (verse 3)?

DA'SCOOP The New Testament was first written in

Greek. And the Greek word for "desires" gives us our word "hedonism," a four-syllable way to say you seek pleasure above everything else in life. The phrase "to spend what you get" is the same label the Bible uses for the way a disobedient son trashed his life and money (Luke 15:14).

Wanting only to satisfy yourself—instead of helping others and pleasing God—is "adulterous." Why such a nasty label (verses 4–5)?

*INSIGHT God is jealous for your love, so James compares selfishness to hopping in bed with someone else's spouse. God wants you to resist the world when it pulls you away from him— into things that are outright evil or even less than best.

Count 'em: James next rattles off ten commands that call for immediate change. His solution in verse 7 sums up all the rest. What is it? What should you do?

*SIDELIGHT Submitting to God is rearranging your desires. It's deciding to want right things for right reasons. God is eager to answer your prayers—*but only if what you want's good*. First John 5:14 relays this foolproof promise: "This is the confidence we have in approaching God: that if we ask anything according to his will, he hears us."

BIG QUESTIONS This Bible Chunk sounds like God has all sorts of stuff to give—but that we don't ask *enough*. What would keep you from going to God for what you need?

Think of the last two or three things you asked God for. What were they? What motivated your requests?

Can you think of things you've asked God for that, looking back, were obviously outside what he'd want to give you? Like what?

*DEEP THOT A no from God doesn't always mean that your desire is selfish. Sometimes he's got something better. And what God really wants to give you is his absolute best. That's what you'll look at next.

STICKY STUFF Use James 4:2–3 to shut down way-selfish desires that wander through your brain.

PRAY ABOUT IT *God, reshape the things I want from you. Help me want right things for right reasons.*

DIG ON Read the rest of that foolproof promise in 1 John 5:14–15.

(4.) Santa's Lap
God's best gift of all

The shopping-mall Santa thought Taysha was way too old to be coming to see him, but she still waited her turn and hopped on his lap. When she pulled out her wish list, it unfurled all the way to the floor. As she ticked through 416 items, Santa winced. "I'll do my best," he said, "but I'll need to do some checking with your mommy and daddy." And as Santa's helpers snapped Taysha's picture, he whispered, "Girl, you've got a bad case of the gimmies."

BRAIN DRAIN If you could ask God for anything, what's the biggest you'd go for?

FLASHBACK Prayer isn't like hopping up on Santa's lap. You're not presenting your wish list to a figment of everyone's imagination. It isn't like having a genie who grants you three wishes and heads back to his lamp. God is too kind to give in to every wish on your list, and his offer to help never vanishes. But here's the best part: God wants to train your tastes so you know enough to ask for the greatest gift he has to give. It's something he promises will totally satisfy you—a promise based on the fact that he knows you inside and out. But how are you supposed to know what this great gift is? See how Jesus helped one woman figure that out.

BIBLE CHUNK Read John 4:4–15

(4) Now he [Jesus] had to go through Samaria. (5) So he came to a town in Samaria called Sychar, near the plot of ground Jacob had given to his

son Joseph. (6) Jacob's well was there, and Jesus, tired as he was from the journey, sat down by the well. It was about the sixth hour.

(7) When a Samaritan woman came to draw water, Jesus said to her, "Will you give me a drink?" (8) (His disciples had gone into the town to buy food.)

(9) The Samaritan woman said to him, "You are a Jew and I am a Samaritan woman. How can you ask me for a drink?" (For Jews do not associate with Samaritans.)

(10) Jesus answered her, "If you knew the gift of God and who it is that asks you for a drink, you would have asked him and he would have given you living water."

(11) "Sir," the woman said, "you have nothing to draw with and the well is deep. Where can you get this living water? (12) Are you greater than our father Jacob, who gave us the well and drank from it himself, as did also his sons and his flocks and herds?"

(13) Jesus answered, "Everyone who drinks this water will be thirsty again, (14) but whoever drinks the water I give him will never thirst. Indeed, the water I give him will become in him a spring of water welling up to eternal life."

(15) The woman said to him, "Sir, give me this water so that I won't get thirsty and have to keep coming here to draw water."

STUFF TO KNOW Jesus meets a woman at a well. He asks for a drink. What does she say (verse 9)?

INSIGHT The culture that surrounded Jesus gave him three reasons to ignore the woman at the well. She was from Samaria— regarded as unspiritual second cousins of God's people. She was a woman—not fit to converse with a male stranger, much less a teacher like Jesus. And she was a sinner—a side of the story that comes out right after the Bible Chunk you read. Yet Jesus talks to her.

Jesus hints that the woman isn't up to speed on two things. What are they (verse 10)?

INSIGHT First, Jesus has a gift to offer her that she knows nothing about. Second, she doesn't realize who he is. He's politely saying, "If you knew who you were talking to—and what I have to offer—you'd ask *me* for a drink."

What beverage does Jesus offer to the woman (verse 10)?

INSIGHT Still hazy, she wonders how he'll get anything out of that swell well. But what's this "living" water? A cup of *E. coli* and other intestinal-busting bacteria? No. Jesus is saying he's the stuff that satisfies—and if you get him, you've got what you need.

Does the woman want what Jesus offers? Does she fully grasp what he's giving? How do you know (verse 15)?

BIG QUESTIONS The biggest thing you can ever ask from God is maybe way bigger than you've ever imagined: It's God himself. *Sooooo* . . . have you ever told God you want more of *him*— not just stuff he can give you?

If you told God right now that you wanted to know him better, would you expect scary surprises—or what?

How would your life be different if you got to know God better—bit by bit, day by day?

DEEP THOT Knowing the biggest thing you can ask God for—and how much better it is than what we usually want—is like wising up to the difference between a fingernail-sized cubic zirconia and a football-sized diamond. One is pretty but plastic. The other is priceless.

STICKY STUFF Quench your thirst with John 4:14.

PRAY ABOUT IT *Jesus, I want more of you—to "see you more clearly" and "follow you more nearly."*

DIG ON Grab the rest of the story of the woman at the well—including the part where the crowds conclude Jesus is the Savior of the world—in John 4:16–42.

5. Come and Get It
Asking according to God's will

"Jesus," Trevor prayed, "I've messed around when people have wanted to tell me about you, and I haven't tried very hard to get to know you. I want to follow you and live like a Christian. But I need you to help me. Can you do that?"

BRAIN DRAIN How do you act when you get serious about being close to God?

FLASHBACK Remember 1 John 5:14? It says "we can be confident that he will listen to us whenever we ask him for anything in line with his will" (NLT). The biggest, don't-miss-it part of God's will is that you grab hold of him and get to know him well. You want that? Ask for it. God guarantees he'll grant it to you. But he also wants you to ask for—and to give you—everything else in his great big will.

BIBLE CHUNK Read Psalm 37:1–6, 23–26, 37–40

(1) Do not fret because of evil men
    or be envious of those who do wrong;
(2) for like the grass they will soon wither,
    like green plants they will soon die away.
(3) Trust in the Lord and do good;
    dwell in the land and enjoy safe pasture.
(4) Delight yourself in the Lord
    and he will give you the desires of your heart.
(5) Commit your way to the Lord;

trust in him and he will do this:

(6) He will make your righteousness shine like the dawn,
the justice of your cause like the noonday sun. . . .

(23) If the Lord delights in a man's way,
he makes his steps firm;

(24) though he stumble, he will not fall,
for the Lord upholds him with his hand.

(25) I was young and now I am old,
yet I have never seen the righteous forsaken
or their children begging bread.

(26) They are always generous and lend freely;
their children will be blessed. . . .

(37) Consider the blameless, observe the upright;
there is a future for the man of peace.

(38) But all sinners will be destroyed;
the future of the wicked will be cut off.

(39) The salvation of the righteous comes from the Lord;
he is their stronghold in time of trouble.

(40) The Lord helps them and delivers them;
he delivers them from the wicked and saves them,
because they take refuge in him.

STUFF TO KNOW Verse 4 says God wants to give you the desires of your heart. There's no catch—but what's the condition? What's the first half of that verse say?

What else does God want you to do (verse 5)?

SIDELIGHT Your "way" is your whole life. You can't claim you're ga-ga about God if you gag on following him. Part of "delighting" in God is heeding his plans for you—that package of plans the Bible calls God's "will." You can think of God's will like this. He has . . .

- an *ultimate* will—that you be a Christian. "God our Savior . . .

wants everyone to be saved and to understand the truth" (1 Timothy 2:3–4 NLT).

- a *universal* will—that you obey the Bible's commands, which God intends for everyone. Jesus said, "You are my friends if you obey me" (John 15:14 NLT).
- a *specific* will—that you live by the step-by-step guidance God gives you through the Bible, prayer, circumstances, and the wise advice, "Seek his will in all you do, and he will direct your paths" (Proverbs 3:6 NLT).

What can you count on God to do when you "commit your way" to him (verses 6, 23–24)?

What kind of needs does God take care of (verse 25)?

BIG QUESTIONS Suppose you decide to totally follow God—to obey in every way you know. What would that be like?

SIDELIGHT Jeremiah 29:11 leaves no doubt how good it is to follow God's map for your life: " 'For I know the plans I have for you,' declares the Lord, 'plans to prosper you and not to harm you, plans to give you hope and a future.' "

What about following God's plans *doesn't* sound like a good idea?

SIDELIGHT When your prayer is to get close to God and live according to God's will, his answers are mind-blowing: "By his mighty power at work within us," the Bible promises, "he is able to accomplish infinitely more than we would ever dare to ask or hope" (Ephesians 3:20 NLT).

You pray. God answers. So how much do you trust God that he really wants to give you his best?

DEEP THOT God doesn't just want to hand you stuff. He wants to walk hand-in-hand with you. When you ask for God's will—whatever it is—you're going to get God's best.

STICKY STUFF If you want to get the desires of your heart, don't forget Psalm 37:4.

PRAY ABOUT IT *God, I want you. And I want all of your will in my life.*

DIG ON Read Psalm 40:7–8, an Old Testament Bible Chunk the New Testament applied to Jesus in Hebrews 10:7.

Talk About It • 1

EMPATHIZE: What's going on in your life?
ENCOURAGE: How are you doing with Jesus?
EQUIP: What one truth will you take home today?

- Do you sweat when people ask you to pray? How come—or not? (Study 1)
- Do you figure it was easy for Moses to talk with God speaking from "within the bush"? Why or why not? (Study 1)
- What do you think of the way Moses talks to God? (Study 1)
- Do you think God is glad to give to you? (Study 2)
- What's the promise of Matthew 7:7? (Study 2)
- If God knows all your needs, why pray? (Study 2)
- What's one huge reason people don't get what they ask for from God? (Study 3)
- What keeps you from going to God for everything you need? (Study 3)
- Have you ever told God you want more of *him*—not just the stuff he can give you? (Study 4)
- If you told God right now that you wanted to know him better, would you expect scary surprises—or what? (Study 4)
- What does God's will have to do with getting what you want? (Study 5)
- You pray. God answers. So how much do you trust God that he really wants to give you his best? (Study 5)

PART 2

NO FAKEY PRAYERS

⑥ How Real People Pray
The Lord's Prayer

A firm grasp on Caleb's shoulder steers him toward the microphone. "They're waiting for you," whispers his youth pastor. Without warning, the crush of praying in front of church transmogrifies the language centers of Caleb's young brain into those of a sixteenth-century English churchman: "Holiest Father who arteth in heaveneth," Caleb croaks, "we thanketh thee for thy trulyeth bounteous gifts unto thee, um, I meaneth *we*, and prayeth thy divine benificent and magnificent blessings on us, thy humbleth servants. Verily and verily, amen."

BRAIN DRAIN What's easy for you about praying? What bugs you about it?

FLASHBACK This next chunk isn't the first time the Bible book of Luke shows Jesus praying. He spoke to his Father when the heavens split open (3:21). He went to a mountain to pray for a whole night (6:12). And he seemed unfazed by praying in front of his disciples (9:28). For someone capable of uttering crowd-wowing prayers, Jesus has a surprising response when his followers say, "Teach us to pray."

BIBLE CHUNK Read Luke 11:1–4

(1) One day Jesus was praying in a certain place. When he finished, one of his disciples said to him, "Lord, teach us to pray, just as John taught his disciples."

(2) He said to them, "When you pray, say:
" 'Father,
hallowed be your name,
your kingdom come.
(3) Give us each day our daily bread.
(4) Forgive us our sins,
for we also forgive everyone who sins against us.
And lead us not into temptation.' "

STUFF TO KNOW What two or three words would you use to describe the prayer Jesus taught (verses 2–4)?

SIDELIGHT That Bible version—or how you say the Lord's Prayer in church—might sound stuffy. Even so, you probably wouldn't expect the Son of God to teach such a shrimpy prayer. And a different translation of the Bible gets Jesus' simple, straightforward tone even better: "Father, may your name be honored. May your Kingdom come soon. Give us our food day by day. And forgive us our sins—just as we forgive those who have sinned against us. And don't let us yield to temptation" (NLT).

So when Jesus says, "Hey-thanks-for-asking-this-is-how-you-should-pray," exactly what kind of stuff does he pray for (2–4)?

DA'SCOOP Lots to catch:

- "Hallowed be your name" asks that God would be regarded as holy—prized for his pure goodness.
- "Your kingdom come" wants people on planet earth to live as God's subjects. The Bible book of Matthew, by the way, also records the phrase "Your will be done on earth as it is in heaven," which gets at the same point (Matthew 6:10).

- "Daily bread" covers the real things you *need*, though maybe not all the stuff you *want*.
- That "forgive us our debts" part doesn't mean "Lord, couldn't *you* please make the money I borrowed from my little sister's piggy bank magically reappear" but "don't hold our *moral* debts against us." It's like saying "forgive us as we forgive others."
- And "lead us not into temptation . . ." requests help in overcoming evil. Matthew records a similar phrase here, "deliver us from the evil one" (Matthew 6:13).

INSIGHT You might be wondering whether Luke whacked
off the last line of the Lord's Prayer you say in church. The part "For yours is the kingdom and the power and the glory forever. Amen" shows up only in some late copies of Bible manuscripts, so many Bible translations add it as a footnote. But it's still good stuff.

BIG QUESTIONS From everything you've learned so
far in life, how do you think you're *supposed* to pray?

How is the way you're supposed to pray the same or different from the sort of prayer Jesus taught?

INSIGHT Some people have noticed that Jesus' prayer has
four parts: *praise* (honoring God), *repentance* (asking for forgiveness), *asking* (the daily bread and dealing with temptation stuff), and *yielding* (telling God you want his will). Put that together, and it spells *pray*. More on those parts of prayer in section 3 of *Pray Hard*.

Rank the following from 1 to 10 (1 = "nothing nastier" and 10 = "can't get enough of it"):

- How do you feel about praying by yourself?

- How about with other people?

- What would make prayer easier for you?

DEEP THOT Jesus shows you what the biggest quality of prayer can be: It's real. It's simple. It can be really simple.

PRAY ABOUT IT *Father, may your name be honored. May your kingdom come soon. Give me food day by day. And forgive my sins—just as I forgive those who have sinned against me. And don't let me yield to temptation.*

STICKY STUFF Lodge Jesus' prayer in Luke 11:2–4 in your long-term memory.

DIG ON Jesus likely taught the Lord's Prayer on many occasions. Peek at Matthew 6:1–15 to see the version recorded there—along with some other wise words on prayer.

⑦ Loud and Proud
Bad Bible prayers, part 1

When Pastor Smith prays, he shouts. He grabs the pulpit so it shakes. He sounds as if he's wired straight to the Holy Ghost. And everyone loves to hear him pray. Ummm . . . except God, that is.

BRAIN DRAIN Of all the people you know, who would win a gold medal in an Olympics of prayer? Why do you think that?

FLASHBACK Prayer can be beautiful, song-like, heartfelt, and heated. But Jesus said that some ultrareligious-sounding prayers aren't worth imitating. In this Bible Chunk two people go to the temple. One is a Pharisee—someone known for keeping rules and doing everything right. The other is an old-time tax collector—a guy who's as bad as bad gets. They both approach God to pray. The Pharisee sees their prayer session as a bit of a contest. And now, may the best pray-er win. . . .

BIBLE CHUNK Read Luke 18:9–14

(9) To some who were confident of their own righteousness and looked down on everybody else, Jesus told this parable: (10) "Two men went up to the temple to pray, one a Pharisee and the other a tax collector. (11) The Pharisee stood up and prayed about himself: 'God, I thank you that I am not like other men—robbers, evildoers, adulterers—or even like this tax collector. (12) I fast twice a week and give a tenth of all I get.'

(13) "But the tax collector stood at a distance. He would not even look up to heaven, but beat his breast and said, 'God, have mercy on me, a sinner.'

(14) "I tell you that this man, rather than the other, went home justified before God. For everyone who exalts himself will be humbled, and he who humbles himself will be exalted."

STUFF TO KNOW Who's Jesus talking to in this Bible Chunk (verse 9)?

Those two guys who show up in the temple to pray—who were they again (verse 10)?

What's the Pharisee say to God (verse 11)?

SIDELIGHT Jesus didn't stop at teaching his early followers how to pray. He told them how *not* to pray, bashing prayer that was proud—and public for the wrong reasons: "But when you pray, do not be like the hypocrites, for they love to pray standing in the synagogues and on the street corners to be seen by men. I tell you the truth, they have received their reward in full" (Matthew 6:5–6).

So what's the tax collector do when he prays? And what does he say?

INSIGHT Anyone back in the Bible would have said tax collectors had plenty to be sorry for. They worked for hated Roman rulers—and not only did they collect the government's due, but they always helped themselves to a heap off the top.

How does God score the two pray-ers? Which one has God's favor—the one who brags he always does right, or the one who admits he's really been wrong (verse 14)?

SIDELIGHT Did you pick the winner? Here's what God is looking for when you pray: Psalm 51:17 says, "God, you will not reject a heart that is broken and sorry for sin" (NCV). And Psalm 101:5 says, "I will not allow people to be proud and look down on others" (NCV). The Pharisee thought his spiritual activities and eloquent words would score bonus points with God. But the tax collector was the one who met God.

BIG QUESTIONS How hard is it for you to pray where others can hear?

So when is it wrong to pray in front of people?

INSIGHT Jesus didn't mean you should never pray in front of people. After all, Jesus often did it himself, and he said that group prayer is a great way to talk to God (Matthew 18:20). But Jesus seemed to pray way more in private than in public. Jesus wants to deflate people who pump up their religion in front of others just to be seen.

Do you think God would have liked the tax collector's prayer even better if he'd prayed longer? Why or why not?

INSIGHT God hates prayers that are *proud*. He dislikes prayers that are *public* for the wrong reason. And he has no need for prayers that are *long*. Jesus had occasions where he prayed all night—but he also bashed prayers that kept going . . . and going . . . and going . . . if they kept going for the wrong reasons: "And when you pray, do not keep on babbling like pagans, for they think they will be heard because of their many words" (Matthew 6:7).

DEEP THOT God deserves your utmost respect. And yet your prayers don't have to be loud, lavish, or long. You're talking to your Father. In fact, you're talking to your Friend (John 15:15).

STICKY STUFF Memorize Jesus' great prayer tips from Matthew 6:5, 7.

PRAY ABOUT IT *God, help me just to talk to you—to tell you what's going on in my head and my heart.*

DIG ON Check out 1 Kings 18, where the prophet Elijah mocks the followers of the fake god Baal for praying loud and long. When their god didn't hear them, they "shouted louder and slashed themselves with swords and spears, as was their custom, until their blood flowed" (1 Kings 18:28).

8. You'd Rather Barf Nails
Bad Bible prayers, part 2

"It's for you. It's Tamara."
"Tell her I don't want to talk to her."
"She says it's important."
"Tell her she can find another friend to lie to."
"She says it's really important."
"Tell her I'd rather barf nails."
"She says she wants to apologize."

BRAIN DRAIN Suppose you have an ugly spat with a friend. What happens to your ability to talk to each other?

FLASHBACK You know that when you fight with a friend you throw up a wall between yourself and that person. When you become out-and-out enemies, your communication quits altogether. What you might not know is that the wrongs we do against other people also get in the way of talking with God—and in a big way. Here's the scoop.

BIBLE CHUNK Read Matthew 5:21–24

(21) "You have heard that it was said to the people long ago, 'Do not murder, and anyone who murders will be subject to judgment.' (22) But I tell you that anyone who is angry with his brother will be subject to judgment. Again, anyone who says to his brother, 'Raca,' is answerable to the Sanhedrin. But anyone who says, 'You fool!' will be in danger of the fire of hell.

(23) "Therefore, if you are offering your gift at the altar and there re-

member that your brother has something against you, (24) leave your gift there in front of the altar. First go and be reconciled to your brother; then come and offer your gift."

STUFF TO KNOW What big wrong does Jesus start off talking about in this Bible Chunk? What would happen to anyone who commits murder (verse 21)?

INSIGHT "Subject to judgment" means "brought to trial" either before God or a human council. Everyone who heard Jesus would have known that the Old Testament punishment for murder was hefty—death, generally. But what Jesus said next was the real surprise.

That same punishment applies to people who do what (verse 22)?

DA'SCOOP "Raca" means "imbecile" or "fool" or "blockhead." "Fool" has that meaning plus it implies more than a dash of wickedness.

Now here's the point about prayer: In verse 23 Jesus pictures someone in the solemn inner court of the temple to worship God. What does Jesus say that person should do before he approaches God?

SIDELIGHT In this Bible Chunk the person getting close to God has made someone mad and needs to make it right. But the instruction cuts both ways. If someone has wronged you and

you stay bitter, that too gets in the way of getting close to God. Mark 11:25 says, "And when you stand praying, if you hold anything against anyone, forgive him, so that your Father in heaven may forgive you your sins."

BIG QUESTIONS Why would it bother God if you're having a fight with someone else? What business is it of his?

SIDELIGHT God is the one who defines right and wrong and who commands you to love. So when you sin you're also striking out at God. Funny thing is, the Bible also says that how you treat people reveals your real attitude toward God: "If someone says, 'I love God,' but hates another Christian, that person is a liar; for if we don't love people we can see, how can we love God, whom we have not seen?" (1 John 4:20 NLT).

Why do you suppose Jesus put being angry with other people on par with murder?

INSIGHT Jesus is speaking in hyped-up language. His point? The rage and cruelty you dish out are at the heart of murder, and that if you do those things you'll answer to God.

If anger and put-downs get in the way of connecting with God, what else might be a problem?

SIDELIGHT Hmmm . . . if you ponder life for any more than a minute you figure out that none of us has any shortage of

reasons to shrink before God. The Bible says that "all have sinned; all fall short of God's glorious standard" (Romans 3:23 NLT). And take a gander at what all of us are before we know Jesus: "Once you were alienated from God and were enemies in your minds because of your evil behavior" (Colossians 1:21). Apart from Jesus, you're an alien. Sin makes you God's enemy and separates you from him.

Sounds like we've all been in a fight with God. So what does the fact that God doesn't tolerate sins of any sort do to your desire to pray?

DEEP THOT Remember how Moses trembled when he walked on holy ground? He was afraid in the presence of a righteous God. Yep, God desires and requires respect. But when you become his friend, you don't have to fear him. The next Bible Chunk will show you how God has opened a way to get right with him—so you can be close to him, now and always.

STICKY STUFF Don't let hang-ups with other people hinder your prayers. Get hold of Matthew 5:23–24.

PRAY ABOUT IT *God, on my own I'm not good enough to talk to you. You are a holy God, the most righteous being in the universe. I don't want to be your enemy.*

DIG ON Read Colossians 1:13–14 for a sneak peek at how God makes us his friends again.

13" He has delivered us from the power of darkness & conveyed us into the kingdom of the Son of His love,
14 In whom we have redemption through His blood, the forgiveness of sins.

2. Total Confidence
Getting access to God

You'd scaled a wall, outwitted an ultrahi-tech intruder detection system, and even managed to distract the sad-excuse-for-a-watch-dog with a well-flung sirloin. Just like you suspected, a sliding door off the patio was open. Once inside the home of your all-time favorite TV star, you stroll casually to the dinner table and take a seat. But getting inside doesn't mean you belong there. And grabbing a seat without an invite doesn't give you a right to dinner.

BRAIN DRAIN If someone asked you why you should be allowed to get close to God and to talk to him, what would you say?

FLASHBACK Bold people belly right up to God. Sensitive types sometimes shrivel with fear. If you want to get near God, you'll want to understand what Jesus did to guarantee you a warm welcome into God's presence. It's the knowledge you need to talk to God with total confidence. This Bible Chunk, by the way, relies on an image from the Old Testament. Once a year—and *only* once a year—the temple's high priest entered into the "Most Holy Place," a special place of God's presence. The high priest's ticket to enter was pretty unusual—the blood of goats and calves sacrificed for the sins of the people (Hebrews 9:12). Later in the Bible, Jesus offered himself as the perfect sacrifice for sin once and for all—and made himself our way to get close to God.

BIBLE CHUNK Read Hebrews 10:19–23

(19) Therefore, brothers, since we have confidence to enter the Most Holy Place by the blood of Jesus, (20) by a new and living way opened for us through the curtain, that is, his body, (21) and since we have a great priest over the house of God, (22) let us draw near to God with a sincere heart in full assurance of faith, having our hearts sprinkled to cleanse us from a guilty conscience and having our bodies washed with pure water. (23) Let us hold unswervingly to the hope we profess, for he who promised is faithful.

STUFF TO KNOW What one word describes the attitude with which you can approach God (verse 19)?

But why? If sin alienates us from God, what did Jesus do that was so special (verse 20)?

SIDELIGHT Christ's blood . . . confidence . . . what's the connection? Well, you've heard that sin makes you God's enemy (Colossians 1:21). But here's some better news: "But now [God] has reconciled you by Christ's physical body through death to present you holy in his sight, without blemish and free from accusation" (Colossians 1:22). Instead of being banned from God's presence, there's a place for you at God's table. And you're welcome anytime.

What kind of window treatment does this Bible Chunk compare Jesus to (verse 20)?

SIDELIGHT Hebrews ain't talking about curtains you'd hang in your house, but the curtain that hid God's presence in the

temple's most holy place. When Jesus died, that curtain miraculously shredded in two, a sign of how he had opened the way to God (Matthew 27:51).

What does verse 21 call Jesus? Any clue of what that means?

DA'SCOOP "Great priest over the house of God" is saying Jesus is the guy who brings the right sacrifice to God, the one sacrifice that could bring forgiveness of sins.

So what can you do "with full assurance" that it's okay? How come (verse 22)?

INSIGHT You've been sprinkled and scrubbed up. "Hearts sprinkled" means Christ has cleaned up your innards. "Bodies washed" is a reference to baptism, which is an outward sign of that inward cleansing.

BIG QUESTIONS Suppose God was throwing a party and you wanted to go. What gets you in?

Do you think it's ugly or unfair that Christ's death is necessary for you to truly talk to God? How come?

INSIGHT God is indeed throwing a party. It's called heaven. But until you admit the wrongness of sin and your need for forgiveness, you're on the wrong side. And you're not just a star-crazed groupie. You've made yourself his enemy, and it's like you're still wearing a load of weapons. If you want to get in, you've got to disarm.

When have you told God that you know that Christ died so you can get clean—and so you can talk to him?

INSIGHT Belief in that fact—that God accepts you because of Christ—is something you might have grown up sure of. Or that you can put a date and time on the moment you first believed. Or that you can tell God right now. It's the most basic part of becoming a Christian.

DEEP THOT We're God's enemies—scared to enter his presence—only if we want to be. Jesus accomplished this for us: "Because of Christ and our faith in him, we can now come fearlessly into God's presence, assured of his glad welcome" (Ephesians 3:12 NLT). That's a guarantee good for eternity. But it's also what lets you talk to God right now—with total confidence.

STICKY STUFF Hebrews 10:19 says why you're always welcome at God's place.

PRAY ABOUT IT *Thank you that Jesus died for my sins, God, so I can talk to you with total confidence—now and forever.*

DIG ON Look at Hebrews 9:1–10:25 to learn more about Christ's perfect sacrifice.

(10) Run to the Throne
God understands you

With the smell of beer and smoke soaking Steffi's clothes, her parents only need a sniff to know where she's been. When they tell her she's grounded, she wails, "I don't drink. I don't smoke. Those are my friends. I want to be with them. They understand me." And when Steffi's parents point out that they were once her age and that they *do* understand, she objects. "You're both old. You have no idea what I'm going through."

BRAIN DRAIN Who would you say best understands you? How do you know?

FLASHBACK This Bible Chunk again refers to Jesus as the "high priest" who acts on our behalf, but it highlights another side of what Jesus does. Jesus is totally God. He possesses total knowledge. So you can be sure he already knows and understands what you go through. But by coming to earth in human flesh (John 1:14), you see proof his all-knowing brain has in-the-body experience. Going to God won't help much if he roars at your problems and tells you to mop up your sorry mess by yourself. Your last Bible Chunk showed you *why you can come to God.* This one shows *why you want to.*

BIBLE CHUNK Read Hebrews 4:14–16

(14) Therefore, since we have a great high priest who has gone through the heavens, Jesus the Son of God, let us hold firmly to the faith we pro-

fess. (15) For we do not have a high priest who is unable to sympathize with our weaknesses, but we have one who has been tempted in every way, just as we are—yet was without sin. (16) Let us then approach the throne of grace with confidence, so that we may receive mercy and find grace to help us in our time of need.

STUFF TO KNOW Where has Jesus gone? What difference would Jesus' residence there make (verse 14)?

SIDELIGHT The Bible teaches that at the end of his time on this planet, Jesus "ascended" to heaven (Acts 1:9–11). He didn't just fly into the sky. Jesus came to earth on a mission, and "after he had provided purification for sins, he sat down at the right hand of the Majesty in heaven" (Hebrews 1:3). He's now back in the control center of the universe, forever on your side—living proof that your sins are forgiven (1 John 2:1–2).

Jesus won't smack you upside the head when you have problems—guaranteed. How does he look at your weaknesses (verse 15)?

How do you know (verse 15)?

SIDELIGHT You might wonder how someone who lived in way-back society could be "tempted in every way, just as we are." Get this: The ancient world was more rude and crude than anything most of us will ever experience. Besides that, Jesus was at the center of a cosmic tug-of-war between good and evil. When he

spent more than a month minus food to devote himself to prayer, Satan suggested he miraculously bake himself some bread. Satan dared him to wow the crowds by leaping from the peak of the temple and letting his Father save him. And Satan coached him to take immediate control of the world—to rule without going to the cross.

If Jesus has been through all this, what good does it do you? What attitude can you have as you run to God's throne (verse 16)?

If you run to God with your problems, what are you going to get (verse 16)?

DA'SCOOP "Mercy" is God's tender grasp of your situation—and his ability to unleash whatever resources it takes to take care of you. "Grace" is all about finding God's favor and forgiveness. Roll the two together, and it means that God will give you exactly what you need.

BIG QUESTIONS When you're trying to explain a problem to someone, how much does it matter that they've actually gone through whatever it is you face?

Do you think Jesus actually understands your temptations and other problems? Why or why not?

How could someone who never sinned really know how bad it can get battling to do the right thing?

INSIGHT Jesus knew an even fiercer battle against sin than the rest of us humans. We usually give up and give in to sin before the fight gets truly grueling. Jesus remained true to God's commands his whole life. But he didn't have it easy.

DEEP THOT God understands you at your neediest, whether you need help with your homework or freedom from sins that overpower you. Ponder these words from a song by Graham Kendrick: "He walked where I walk. He stood where I stand. He felt what I feel. He understands."

STICKY STUFF Hebrews 4:16 reminds you that you've always got a friend ready to help.

PRAY ABOUT IT *God, I trust you with my biggest difficulties because you know me inside and out.*

DIG ON Want to find out about the gargantuan temptations Jesus faced? Read about them in Matthew 4:1–11.

Talk About It • 2

EMPATHIZE: What's going on in your life?
ENCOURAGE: How are you doing with Jesus?
EQUIP: What one truth will you take home today?

- What's easy for you about praying? What bugs you about it? (Study 6)
- How would you describe the prayer that Jesus taught his disciples? (Study 6)
- What would make prayer easier for you? (Study 6)
- What kind of prayers does Jesus bash? Whose prayers did he have a problem with? (Studies 7 and 8)
- Why would it bother God if you are having a fight with someone else? (Study 8)
- So what does the fact that God doesn't tolerate sins of any sort do to your desire to pray? (Study 8)
- But how do you know you're welcomed to get near to God in prayer? (Study 9)
- What does Jesus' death have to do with being able to talk to God with total confidence? (Study 9)
- If you run to God with your problems, what are you going to get? (Study 10)
- Do you think Jesus actually understands your temptations and other problems? Why or why not? (Study 10)

PART 3

PARTS OF PRAYER

11. What Have You Got That Isn't a Gift?

Prayer is praise

Here's what we've settled so far about prayer: God has a wild desire to meet your needs. He wants you to ask for right things for right reasons. Getting to know him is the biggest thing you could ask for. He has a whole huge will he wants to give you. Prayer doesn't need to be loud, lavish, or long. God deserves respect, but he invites you to come to him boldly because you belong to him. . . . And now we'll peel away at the big parts of prayer—*praise* (honoring God), *repentance* (asking for forgiveness), *asking* (that's the easy part), and *yielding* (telling God you want what he wants).

BRAIN DRAIN When have you been so excited you screamed out loud?

FLASHBACK Some preachers say that if you yell at football games then you should cheer for God in church. Then again, at football games girls spit peanut shells and guys paint their chests in team colors. But you get their point. The thought of "praising God" might seem flaky or fakey, gaggy or gross. Yet it's the first big part of prayer. And if you've got reason to speak highly of God, you've got something to say straight to God's face. Israel's King David sang these words when God spared him from his biggest enemies.

BIBLE CHUNK Read Psalm 18:25–36

(25) To the faithful you show yourself faithful,
   to the blameless you show yourself blameless,
(26) to the pure you show yourself pure,
   but to the crooked you show yourself shrewd.
(27) You save the humble
   but bring low those whose eyes are haughty.
(28) You, O Lord, keep my lamp burning;
   my God turns my darkness into light.
(29) With your help I can advance against a troop;
   with my God I can scale a wall.
(30) As for God, his way is perfect;
   the word of the Lord is flawless.
   He is a shield
   for all who take refuge in him.
(31) For who is God besides the Lord?
   And who is the Rock except our God?
(32) It is God who arms me with strength
   and makes my way perfect.
(33) He makes my feet like the feet of a deer;
   he enables me to stand on the heights.
(34) He trains my hands for battle;
   my arms can bend a bow of bronze.
(35) You give me your shield of victory,
   and your right hand sustains me;
   you stoop down to make me great.
(36) You broaden the path beneath me,
   so that my ankles do not turn.

STUFF TO KNOW When you look at this Bible
Chunk, it's easy to see David's praises sort into at least three slots:
praise for what God does *for* you, praise for what God does *in* you,
and praise for *who God is*.

First off, spot the stuff God does *for* David:

- How does God care for people who know him (verses 25–27)?

- How does God take care of people who don't follow him
  (verses 25–27)?

- What light does God flip on? What's that mean (verse 28)?

- Where does God let David hide (verse 30)?

- What does God do to smooth out life (verse 36)?

Look at the stuff God does *in* David:

- How strong does he make him (verse 34)?

- Where does God help him hang out (verse 33)?

INSIGHT David's not talking about your modern compound bow with an easy forty-five-pound draw. God is going to make him strong enough to bend pipe with his bare hands. Actually, bronze is a vivid way to say *reeeeallly* strong. Bows were always made out of wood. And that "deer" is a breed whose agility lets it walk on skinny ledges in mountainous, rocky terrain.

And now see some praise-ful words about *God himself*:

- What does David think of how God acts—his "way" (verse 30)?

- What's the one word that describes God's Word (verse 30)?

- Does God have any competitors (verse 31)?

BIG QUESTIONS So has God done anything *for* you—things big or little you can thank him for? What are they?

Has God done anything *in* you—made you better than you'd have been if you hadn't been hooked up with him? Details!

And what about God do you find so spectacular that you want to tell him straight up about it?

DEEP THOT In the New Testament Paul quizzed the

church in Corinth, "What do you have that God hasn't given you?" (1 Corinthians 4:7 NLT). If everything good that you've got is a gift from God, you've got something to praise him for. And because he's the kind of God who gives you good gifts, he's worth praising just because of who he is.

STICKY STUFF Bang Psalm 18:31 around in your
brain—and let it slip past your lips. That's praise.

PRAY ABOUT IT No ready-made prayer this time. Talk
to God about your Big Question lists of praise-worthy items.

DIG ON Check Luke 19:37–40 to see who will praise God if
you don't.

(12.) Come Clean
Prayer is repentance

Jake told his parents he wasn't sure how it happened. But even that was a lie. Instead of driving straight home from school he swung by a friend's house. And he let that friend ride with him. And he was driving too fast. And he was tweaking the stereo. So even though his recollection of the accident was still blurry, Jake knew he hadn't been paying attention to his driving. And how he was going to admit all this to his parents was flipping through his brain as violently as the car had rolled off the road.

BRAIN DRAIN When have you had to say you're sorry—big-time sorry?

FLASHBACK Back in the Old Testament the prophet Nathan shrewdly confronted King David after he had committed adultery with another man's wife. David had a lot to be sorry for. Not only had he taken Bathsheba as his own, but he permanently put her husband out of the picture by having him killed in battle (2 Samuel 11–12). Repentance—the R in PRAY—isn't just saying you're sorry. It's having a total change of mind about your sin, deciding you don't want to live that way anymore. Have a look at David's prayer of repentance, one of the best-known chunks of the Bible.

BIBLE CHUNK Read Psalm 51:1–12

> (1) Have mercy on me, O God,
>   according to your unfailing love;

according to your great compassion
blot out my transgressions.
(2) Wash away all my iniquity
and cleanse me from my sin.
(3) For I know my transgressions,
and my sin is always before me.
(4) Against you, you only, have I sinned
and done what is evil in your sight,
so that you are proved right when you speak
and justified when you judge.
(5) Surely I was sinful at birth,
sinful from the time my mother conceived me.
(6) Surely you desire truth in the inner parts;
you teach me wisdom in the inmost place.
(7) Cleanse me with hyssop, and I will be clean;
wash me, and I will be whiter than snow.
(8) Let me hear joy and gladness;
let the bones you have crushed rejoice.
(9) Hide your face from my sins
and blot out all my iniquity.
(10) Create in me a pure heart, O God,
and renew a steadfast spirit within me.
(11) Do not cast me from your presence
or take your Holy Spirit from me.
(12) Restore to me the joy of your salvation
and grant me a willing spirit, to sustain me.

STUFF TO KNOW What's the first thing David asks God for (verse 1)?

What does David count on to motivate God's forgiveness (verses 1–2)?

SIDELIGHT In the Old Testament, sacrifices and ritual washing symbolized God's removing sin and pulling people back to him. The New Testament says God does an even more thorough

scrubbing-up. He has "saved us through the washing of rebirth and renewal by the Holy Spirit" (Titus 3:5).

Does David get honest about his guilt? How do you know (verses 1–3)?

DA'SCOOP David uses three different words for the sin he's been in. "Transgression" is an act of rebellion and disloyalty. "Iniquity" usually means sinning on purpose. Plain old "sin" is an act that misses a command God has made totally clear. David has blown it and he knows it.

Interesting point: Whom does David say he's wronged (verse 4)?

INSIGHT David slept with Bathsheba and killed off her husband. Yet he regards his wrong against them as an even bigger wrong against God.

Now that David has confessed his sin to God, what kind of heart does he want (verses 10, 12)?

BIG QUESTIONS Do you think only whopper sins like adultery and murder are worth admitting to God?

SIDELIGHT Jesus bulldozed you a path to God. But you'll put a roadblock between you and God if you let "little" sins pile up. If you think you're guiltless, 1 John 1:8 hits you hard: "If we say we have no sin, we are only fooling ourselves and refusing to accept the truth." The next verse, though, tells you how to get hold of God's forgiveness: "But if we confess our sins to him, he is faithful and just to forgive us and to cleanse us from every wrong" (1 John 1:9 NLT).

What gets in the way of you admitting you've done wrong—and asking God to wipe that sin away?

SIDELIGHT You might not see your own wrongdoing. But if you ask God to keep you honest with yourself, he will kindly, gently point out your shortcomings. Pray this prayer from Psalm 139:23–24: "Search me, O God, and know my heart; test me and know my thoughts. Point out anything in me that offends you, and lead me along the path of everlasting life" (NLT).

DEEP THOT "I was wrong" might be three words you seldom say. But if you can't admit when you've sinned, maybe you don't understand why you need Jesus. Prayer is your chance to come clean before God.

STICKY STUFF Psalm 51:10, 12 contains words you might need when you spill your guts to God.

PRAY ABOUT IT *Have mercy on me, O God, according to your unfailing love. Create in me a pure heart, O God, and renew a steadfast spirit within me.*

DIG ON Read about David's admission of guilt in 2 Samuel 12:1–13.

(13.) Soda Pop
Prayer is asking

Prayer is like plunking your money into a pop machine, no? Lots of times you get an immediate *kerkerkerplunk . . . phhhhtt . . . aaah* as you obtain exactly what you aimed for. Other times a sign lights up that says, "Nope. Make another selection." And that nervous twitch you get between punching a button and getting your soda, when you wonder if the machine ate your money, well, that's just like waiting for an answer. Actually, that's where the similarities end. See, you're not dealing with a machine. You're dealing with God.

BRAIN DRAIN When have you asked God for something and not gotten what you wanted right away? How'd you feel?

FLASHBACK Asking is the A in PRAY—and you'd think it would be the easy part of prayer. You've heard you should do your best to aim for right things for right reasons. So you try to figure out the good things God wants for you. But when you put in your prayer and God doesn't *insta-presto* send what you're expecting, you start to wonder where he is—even if he still cares for you. But asking isn't only about getting. It's about trusting.

BIBLE CHUNK Read Psalm 77:1–14

(1) I cried out to God for help; I cried out to God to hear me.
(2) When I was in distress, I sought the Lord;
at night I stretched out untiring hands
and my soul refused to be comforted.

(3) I remembered you, O God, and I groaned;
    I mused, and my spirit grew faint.
    Selah
(4) You kept my eyes from closing;
    I was too troubled to speak.
(5) I thought about the former days,
    the years of long ago;
(6) I remembered my songs in the night.
    My heart mused and my spirit inquired:
(7) "Will the Lord reject forever?
    Will he never show his favor again?
(8) Has his unfailing love vanished forever?
    Has his promise failed for all time?
(9) Has God forgotten to be merciful?
    Has he in anger withheld his compassion?"
    Selah
(10) Then I thought, "To this I will appeal:
    the years of the right hand of the Most High."
(11) I will remember the deeds of the Lord;
    yes, I will remember your miracles of long ago.
(12) I will meditate on all your works
    and consider all your mighty deeds.
(13) Your ways, O God, are holy.
    What god is so great as our God?
(14) You are the God who performs miracles;
    you display your power among the peoples.

STUFF TO KNOW Psalm 77 was written by an Old

Testament musician named Asaph. No one is sure, by the way, if that "selah" thing means "pause" or "crank it up" or "play it again." But what kind of shape is Asaph in when he starts to pray? Who does he hope will help him (verses 1–3)?

Asaph remembers God. What happens? Is that what you'd expect when you think hard about God (verse 3)?

Asaph doesn't fill in the details, but what does it sound like the old days were like (verses 5 and following)?

Asaph's waiting for the pop to drop. What's he worried about (verses 7–9)?

Okay—after all this, does Asaph understand any better where God's long-awaited answer is? So what calms him down (verses 10–14)?

INSIGHT Asking all night long doesn't bring Asaph rest. By remembering God's long history of helping him and other people—with deeds that were 100 percent genuine, 100 percent kind—he finally finds hope. Asaph tells God what he wants. And then he decides to wait—and to trust.

BIG QUESTIONS How do you feel when you have to wait for an answer to prayer?

Think of events in your life—big or small—where you can look back and say, "God took care of me." You were sick and God made you well. You were sad and God cheered you up. You were really needy and God met your need. Got any like that? What could recalling those things do for you when obvious answers to your prayers don't come right away?

INSIGHT Everything good in your life is from God (James 1:17). But Asaph didn't just dig back to the details of his own life to see God's care. He thought back to the big miracles God had pulled off to help his people. He found concrete reasons for trusting God.

DEEP THOT God is way more than a soda machine. He's the all-knowing, all-loving Being who responds to your requests one by one, all to give you the right gifts at the right time. So ask and keep on asking. But remember when it's time to trust.

STICKY STUFF Psalm 77:11–12 will help your heart believe God will give you his best in his good time.

PRAY ABOUT IT *God, help me be bold enough to ask you for everything I need. Help me be patient enough to wait for your best answers.*

DIG ON Psalm 31:14–15 tells you that God is worth trusting—and that you're on his schedule.

(14.) Nothing Better
Prayer is yielding

Justin leaned against the door to his favorite teacher's classroom. A tear slid down his cheek. "My dad's cancer," he choked, "is back." Only in the past few days had Justin realized his dad's sickness was way worse than he'd thought—and that his dad was unlikely to live. As his teacher reached out to hug him, Justin kicked the door hard. *God, you can't let him die*, he thought. *I need my dad.*

BRAIN DRAIN What's the biggest, most important thing you've ever asked for from God—and he said no?

FLASHBACK In this Bible Chunk Jesus prayed knowing it was his Father's will that he die as the sacrificial, wrath-absorbing Passover Lamb—a death more hideous than any of us will ever face. Even while Jesus questioned whether there was some other way to save the world, his goal was to be smack in the center of God's will—even when it included suffering. "Yielding" is what you do when you're driving and you give the other person the right of way. It's giving in. It's going God's way. Sometimes it's saying, "I don't understand, but I want it your way, God." Yielding is the Y in PRAY.

BIBLE CHUNK Read Matthew 26:36–46

(36) Then Jesus went with his disciples to a place called Gethsemane, and he said to them, "Sit here while I go over there and pray." (37) He took Peter and the two sons of Zebedee along with him, and he began to be

sorrowful and troubled. (38) Then he said to them, "My soul is over-whelmed with sorrow to the point of death. Stay here and keep watch with me."

(39) Going a little farther, he fell with his face to the ground and prayed, "My Father, if it is possible, may this cup be taken from me. Yet not as I will, but as you will."

(40) Then he returned to his disciples and found them sleeping. "Could you men not keep watch with me for one hour?" he asked Peter. (41) "Watch and pray so that you will not fall into temptation. The spirit is willing, but the body is weak."

(42) He went away a second time and prayed, "My Father, if it is not possible for this cup to be taken away unless I drink it, may your will be done."

(43) When he came back, he again found them sleeping, because their eyes were heavy. (44) So he left them and went away once more and prayed the third time, saying the same thing.

(45) Then he returned to the disciples and said to them, "Are you still sleeping and resting? Look, the hour is near, and the Son of Man is be-trayed into the hands of sinners. (46) Rise, let us go! Here comes my be-trayer!"

STUFF TO KNOW How is Jesus feeling? Who gets picked to go with him (verse 37)?

INSIGHT Jesus picks his three closest followers—Peter, James, and John. He wants their support as he faces "a sorrow so deep it almost kills."

What does Jesus ask these guys to do (verse 38)? How well do they perform (verses 40, 43, 45)?

And what does Jesus ask his Father (verse 39)?

INSIGHT "This cup" isn't just about Christ's physical suffering and death on the cross. It was his becoming the sacrifice for our total sins—and the brunt of God's wrath. Jesus wondered whether it was possible for him to save the world some other way.

If it wasn't possible for "this cup to be taken from me," what did Jesus want (verse 39)?

BIG QUESTIONS Now, this is weird. Jesus is absolutely one with the Father. But he still struggles with his Father's will. Can *he* do that? Can *you* do that?

INSIGHT Jesus knows that if he obeys his Father his immediate future will be zero fun. And he shows what it means to ask and keep on asking—and to yield: *He asks for "yes" until his Father makes clear his answer is "no." And then he agrees to go God's way.*

Jesus knew why he had to die. Loads of times God's reasons for saying "no" to us aren't so obvious. How easy or hard is it for you to choose God's will when you don't get what's going on?

SIDELIGHT God always gives what's good to those who trust him. But that doesn't mean we always grasp God's reasoning. It's hard to hear God say no whether your request is big or little. It's really hard to hear people's too-easy explanations of why God, for example, doesn't heal someone you love. From the mouth of someone who's been there: In 2 Corinthians 12:7–10 Paul tells how he prayed three times for God to take away a "thorn," likely an opponent or a serious physical ailment. Paul didn't get what he wanted. One thing Paul did receive: a hunk of God's power that was big enough to see him through his suffering.

DEEP THOT You have a good idea of what's good in your life. And you can pray hard for it, doing that "ask and keep on asking" thing. Thing is, only God sees who truly wants his help. Only God knows how each of us can best reach his ultimate goal—that we know him well. And so only God can decide exactly what is best. Like Jesus, sometimes we struggle to accept this fact: When we get God's will, we get God's best.

STICKY STUFF Matthew 26:39 shows you that even Jesus had times he struggled to want his Father's will.

PRAY ABOUT IT *In everything I pray, God, I want your way.*

DIG ON Second Samuel 12:15–23 shows Israel's king David wrestling with God for an answer—and yielding at the right time.

15. Say It Again, Sam
Remembering to thank God

When Teresa's favorite aunt and uncle pulled into the driveway, she wanted to slither under the sofa. For her birthday they'd sent her a gift certificate to her favorite store. She spent the gift in a flash, but she never wrote a thank-you—or told them what she'd bought. Teresa knew her aunt and uncle would never call her an ungrateful little swine. But they were so nice . . . and kind . . . and giving . . . and she forgot.

BRAIN DRAIN What's something in your life that's caused you to spout something like "thankyouthankyouthankyou"?

FLASHBACK You don't say thanks just to ease the pressure on your guilty brain. It's the right thing to do when anyone— God included—has given you a gift. But as you'll see in this Bible Chunk, saying thanks also causes something good to happen in *you*. The group of guys here have a skin ailment—leprosy, now known as Hansen's Disease—that was untreatable until only a generation ago.

BIBLE CHUNK Read Luke 17:11–19

(11) Now on his way to Jerusalem, Jesus traveled along the border between Samaria and Galilee. (12) As he was going into a village, ten men who had leprosy met him. They stood at a distance (13) and called out in a loud voice, "Jesus, Master, have pity on us!"

(14) When he saw them, he said, "Go, show yourselves to the priests." And as they went, they were cleansed.

(15) One of them, when he saw he was healed, came back, praising God in a loud voice. (16) He threw himself at Jesus' feet and thanked him—and he was a Samaritan.

(17) Jesus asked, "Were not all ten cleansed? Where are the other nine? (18) Was no one found to return and give praise to God except this foreigner?" (19) Then he said to him, "Rise and go; your faith has made you well."

STUFF TO KNOW What do those folks call Jesus? Are you impressed by their spiritual insight and respect (verse 13)?

What exactly do these guys ask for (verse 13)?

So what do the men with leprosy get when they act on Jesus' command (verse 14)?

INSIGHT Only a miraculous, total healing would allow someone suffering from leprosy back into society (Numbers 12:9–15). The disease disfigured their bodies and made them unclean outcasts. Jesus sends them to the priests for an official skin checkup.

Someone comes back. Who? Why? What's he do and say (verses 15–16)?

Jesus wonders something. What (verses 17–18)?

INSIGHT Notice: Like the woman at the well you read about a while back, the main character in this chunk is a Samaritan, an unspiritual cousin of the people of Israel. People wouldn't have expected the guy they deemed a spiritual slob to say thanks.

What did Jesus expect of the other nine guys (verse 17)?

SIDELIGHT When you live close to God you start to ooze thankfulness. First Thessalonians 5:18 says to "give thanks in all circumstances, for this is God's will for you in Christ Jesus." Psalm 107:8 (NCV) says what to say thanks for even if you forget everything else: "Give thanks to the Lord for his love and for the miracles he does for people."

You can bet those other guys didn't grumble at the gift they got. Yet only one came back to openly thank Jesus for healing his disease. What does Jesus say has happened in the single guy who said thanks (verse 19)?

INSIGHT Bonus! In verse 14, the leper already had been "cleansed." But get this: In verse 19 Jesus uses a bigger, more complete word that means "made well." Besides receiving a physical healing, this guy got a side benefit. He had something good happening in his heart. Some Bible buffs think he became a full-fledged follower of Jesus.

BIG QUESTIONS What goes through your head when someone gives you something great? How easy is it for you to think about the giver—and not just the gift?

How do you feel when you say thanks in the right way and at the right time? What's it do for you?

DEEP THOT What are you going to say *after* you P-R-A-Y? *After* God has answered—whatever that answer is? Give thanks to the One who gives you everything you've got! If God is the giver of anything good you've got—*everything* from material possessions to talents to friends and family—it's time to "enter his gates with thanksgiving and his courts with praise; give thanks to him and praise his name" (Psalm 100:4).

STICKY STUFF Scarf down 1 Thessalonians 5:18 and remember to say thanks.

PRAY ABOUT IT *Thanks, God, for everything you've given me.*

DIG ON Psalm 136 has a stack of reasons to say thanks.

Talk About It • 3

EMPATHIZE: What's going on in your life?
ENCOURAGE: How are you doing with Jesus?
EQUIP: What one truth will you take home today?

- What has God done *for* you that you can thank him for? (Study 11)
- Has God done anything *in* you—made you better than you'd have been if you hadn't been hooked up with him? What? (Study 11)
- What about God do you find so spectacular that you want to tell him about it? (Study 11)
- What gets in the way of admitting you've done wrong—and asking God to wipe that sin away? (Study 12)
- Explain what 1 John 1:8–9 says. (Study 12)
- When have you asked God for something and not gotten what you wanted right away? How'd you feel? (Study 13)
- So what are you supposed to do while you wait for God's answers? (Study 13)
- What's the biggest, most important thing you've asked God for—and he said no? (Study 14)
- Jesus struggled with his Father's will. Can *he* do that? Can *you* do that? (Study 14)
- How do you feel when you say thanks in the right way and at the right time? What's it do for you? (Study 15)

PART 4

BIGGIE
THINGS
TO PRAY
FOR

(16.) Stoopid to Sweat
Giving God your worries

You wake three hours before your alarm is set to go off. T-minus four hours until the start of standardized tests. You can hear yourself sweat. See, your teachers claim that if you don't pass, then you get an automatic boot to summer school—or worse. You've heard that last year some really smart kid pulled out two fistfuls of hair, flung them in the air, and bolted away screaming. You're wondering if you should save everyone's time and tattoo "STOOPID" across your forehead right now.

BRAIN DRAIN How do you cope when life hurls hard stuff at you?

FLASHBACK In the next five chunks you'll see five biggie things you won't want to miss when you pray—like handing God stuff that slaps you, getting guidance to navigate life, helping out your too-weird world, and spreading God's Good News. And one last chunk reminds you to take time to listen to God too.

Now, nothing prods you to pray like the ugly situations of everyday life, though you might want to work on making God the first place you run—instead of the last. The Bible makes the promise of God's care clear. You can "Give all your worries and cares to God, for he cares about what happens to you" (1 Peter 5:7 NLT).

BIBLE CHUNK Read Psalm 5:1–12

(1) Give ear to my words, O Lord,
consider my sighing.

(2) Listen to my cry for help,
   my King and my God,
   for to you I pray.

(3) In the morning, O Lord, you hear my voice;
   in the morning I lay my requests before you
   and wait in expectation.

(4) You are not a God who takes pleasure in evil;
   with you the wicked cannot dwell.

(5) The arrogant cannot stand in your presence;
   you hate all who do wrong.

(6) You destroy those who tell lies;
   bloodthirsty and deceitful men the Lord abhors.

(7) But I, by your great mercy,
   will come into your house;
   in reverence will I bow down toward your holy temple.

(8) Lead me, O Lord, in your righteousness
   because of my enemies—make straight your way before me.

(9) Not a word from their mouth can be trusted;
   their heart is filled with destruction.
   Their throat is an open grave;
   with their tongue they speak deceit.

(10) Declare them guilty, O God!
   Let their intrigues be their downfall.
   Banish them for their many sins,
   for they have rebelled against you.

(11) But let all who take refuge in you be glad;
   let them ever sing for joy.
   Spread your protection over them,
   that those who love your name may rejoice in you.

(12) For surely, O Lord, you bless the righteous;
   you surround them with your favor as with a shield.

STUFF TO KNOW David's up early to pray. What's he want God to hear (verses 1–2)?

Once David lays out his requests, what's he do next (verse 3)?

Why do you suppose David launches into a lecture on God's dislike of evil (verses 4–6)?

How does David expect to get into God's presence (verse 7)?

INSIGHT God totally hates evil. And people who do evil can't stand in his presence. David counts on God's "mercy," a trait that can also be translated as "unfailing love." It's that grace that became really obvious at Christ's death, the invite that lets you run boldly into God's presence.

What does David want God to do to his enemies? Think it's okay to pray that way (verses 9–11)?

INSIGHT Maybe you've prayed, "Roast them, O God" over some of your enemies. Lots of the prayers of the Bible—especially the Psalms—tell God how rotten life is. They demand that God do something about the evil he hates. It's a fair prayer. But notice this: It trusts God to do the punishing.

BIG QUESTIONS What do you think of what David does with his worries?

SIDELIGHT Philippians 4:6–7 tells you what to do to whatever wallops you: "Don't worry about anything; instead, pray about everything. Tell God what you need, and thank him for all he has done. If you do this, you will experience God's peace, which is far more wonderful than the human mind can understand. His peace will guard your hearts and minds as you live in Christ Jesus" (NLT).

What—or who—is the biggest worry in your life right now?

What would you like to tell God about the stuff that makes you wake up sweating?

DEEP THOT Life is hurting David. He's desperate for God to act. And he tells God all about it. That's what you can do with worry.

STICKY STUFF Psalm 5:1–2 gives you words to pray through life's tough stuff.

PRAY ABOUT IT Tell God about something that's bugging you.

DIG ON Read what Jesus says about worry in Matthew 6:25–34.

17. Whamming the Wall
Asking God for guidance

Shawn's mother frowns. "You can't do everything, you know," she tells him. But Shawn knows that. He's doing well playing sax, but his homework has been getting harder all year. His mom says that missing Tuesday nights at church isn't an option. But he's still stuck between trying out for the school play and playing basketball again. And he'd really like to get a paper route or do something to make some money. His older sister says, "Just figure it out," like it's all so obvious. And his older brother says, *"Pooooor baaaby,"* like his choices are no big deal. So what to do?

BRAIN DRAIN What's the biggest decision you face in the next six months? How will you make your choice?

FLASHBACK You maybe remember that God has an *ultimate* will for you—that you be a Christian. A *universal* will—that you heed all those commands God utters that apply to everybody. And a *specific* will—that you discover the one-of-a-kind plan he has for you. God makes his ultimate will and universal will blazingly clear in the Bible. But if you want his specific will in the nitty-gritty picks of life, you'll want to ask him for wisdom.

BIBLE CHUNK Read James 1:2–8

(2) Consider it pure joy, my brothers, whenever you face trials of many kinds, (3) because you know that the testing of your faith develops perseverance. (4) Perseverance must finish its work so that you may be mature

and complete, not lacking anything. (5) If any of you lacks wisdom, he should ask God, who gives generously to all without finding fault, and it will be given to him. (6) But when he asks, he must believe and not doubt, because he who doubts is like a wave of the sea, blown and tossed by the wind. (7) That man should not think he will receive anything from the Lord; (8) he is a double-minded man, unstable in all he does.

STUFF TO KNOW
Picture this: You're humming through life when suddenly you wham into something. How are you supposed to react when you face a trial (verse 2)?

Is this crazy or what? Tough times make most people feel miserable. Why get glad (verses 3–4)?

DA'SCOOP
A "trial" is anything that puts you to the test—either from the outside, like persecution, or from the inside, like temptation. "Perseverance" is the ability to stand firm, staying on your feet in a storm. "Mature and complete" means you attain all the cool stuff God plans for you.

So you're in this brutal-but-beneficial experience. What do you need to make it through (verse 5)?

INSIGHT
The grammar here assumes that if you're hung up in the middle of a trial—in other words, if you're experiencing life's normal knocks—you need help of the step-by-step kind. You need wisdom to know where to head. And help in getting there.

SIDELIGHT If you're looking for wisdom, there's no better place to go than to the Totally Wise One. Look at Proverbs 3:5–7: "Trust in the Lord with all your heart; do not depend on your own understanding. Seek his will in all you do, and he will direct your paths. Don't be impressed with your own wisdom. Instead, fear the Lord and turn your back on evil" (NLT).

Suppose you turn to God for help. What's his attitude as he doles out his wise guidance (verse 5)?

INSIGHT Remember? You've got a God who knows exactly what you're facing. God gives wisdom "generously" and "without finding fault." Translation: He's happy to guide you. And he won't make you feel stupid.

Ummm. . . . what's the one thing that could get in your way of getting guidance from God (verses 6–7)?

INSIGHT God wants to give wisdom to people who are listening—and in Bible terms, listening means being ready to obey. Being "doubleminded" means half your brain is saying, "I want God's guidance!" and the other half is saying, "I want to do my own thing!" God wants you to expect him to give you guidance. And even before you know what his guidance is, tell God you'll obey.

BIG QUESTIONS Think of that whopper decision that looms over you. If you're going to figure out what to do, what kind of specific wisdom do you need from God?

When you ask God for wisdom, how do you expect him to respond?

INSIGHT That's a huge topic—one I co-wrote a book about with Josh McDowell called *God's Will, God's Best*. But here's the quickie answer: God will direct you through the Bible, through circumstances, and through the wise advice of other people. But the process starts with prayer. Lay out your needs and God will figure out how to light your way.

DEEP THOT The biggest thing you need from God often isn't a thing. It's his wise guidance. When you ask, you'll get wisdom. Not wisecracks.

STICKY STUFF Jam James 1:5 into your brain juice.

PRAY ABOUT IT Talk to God about some areas where you need guidance, now and down the road.

DIG ON The Bible has more wise words about wisdom in James 4:13–16. It talks about the flip side of not knowing what to do—thinking you know so much you don't need God.

(18.) Dream On
Praying for big stuff

When Savana's youth pastor suggests she pray for a teacher she dislikes, she thinks he surely must speak in jest. "It's right here," he says as he thumbs through his Bible. "There's not a lot you can do to change the guy, but at least you can pray for him," he argues. "Yeah," Savana smiles, "I'll pray he won't be so boring."

BRAIN DRAIN Who's the last person on your list of people you'd be utterly thrilled to pray for?

FLASHBACK It's hard to spot in the section you'll read, but the big topic of this next Bible Chunk is group worship. It's an argument that prayer should be way up on the list of things we do at Christian gatherings—especially prayer for people in authority. The point of this passage isn't to scare you off from talking to God on your own. But the kind of prayers covered here are big-issue, community concerns—and it takes all of us to wrap our prayers around them.

BIBLE CHUNK Read 1 Timothy 2:1–8

(1) I urge, then, first of all, that requests, prayers, intercession and thanksgiving be made for everyone—(2) for kings and all those in authority, that we may live peaceful and quiet lives in all godliness and holiness. (3) This is good, and pleases God our Savior, (4) who wants all men to be saved and to come to a knowledge of the truth. (5) For there is one God and one mediator between God and men, the man Christ Jesus, (6) who gave himself as a ransom for all men—the testimony given in its proper

time. (7) And for this purpose I was appointed a herald and an apostle—I am telling the truth, I am not lying—and a teacher of the true faith to the Gentiles.

(8) I want men everywhere to lift up holy hands in prayer, without anger or disputing.

STUFF TO KNOW Paul starts by rattling off four varieties of prayer. What are they (verse 1)?

DA'SCOOP "Request" is telling God your needs and desires. "Prayer" is the broadest word, meaning talking to God either in public or private. "Intercession" implies prayer should be a conversation with God—it's that idea that you can boldly get close to God, all wrapped up in a single word. And "thanksgiving" reminds you to show gratitude for what God has already done for you.

Pray for whom? Is Paul serious (verses 1–2)?

INSIGHT Pray for "everyone" sounds pretty broad. But Paul especially highlights praying for people in authority. You might not have a king in your life, but it's likely you've got a president or a prime minister on top of a principal and a teacher or two.

Look at the gargantuan result of these prayers:

- What good does praying for people in authority do for us (verse 2)?

- What good does it do for people who don't know God (verses 3–4)?

That's a big payoff. But it's part of God's plan. See why: What's God's goal for the human race (verse 4)?

How huge of a commitment has God made to make that happen (verses 5–6)?

INSIGHT The word for "ransom" means Christ paid the price to set the whole world free from sin. In other words, he bought us. He owns us.

One more time: What does all this add up to—and it goes for girls and guys, not just "men" (verse 8)?

BIG QUESTIONS Who in your life qualifies as an "everyone" you're to pray for? What kind of stuff would be helpful to them? What can you ask God to give them?

Name two or three authorities in your life. What could you pray for them?

So what if you think the big guys and gals you're supposed to pray for are bozos?

INSIGHT At the time Paul wrote this letter the head of the Roman empire was the monster Nero. Considering the fact that Nero later killed Paul, this is a money-where-your-mouth-is model of praying for people you don't like—no matter how strange it seems.

DEEP THOT God wants his love to reach every person on the planet. People in authority can help or hinder his plan. When an authority gets in the way—or just gets on your nerves— the solution seldom is to rebel. It's to pray.

STICKY STUFF Use 1 Timothy 2:1–2 to remember to pray for people who rule you.

PRAY ABOUT IT Pray that the authorities in your life would lead well—and that they would help your life, not harm it.

DIG ON If you think praying for authorities is way out, look at what Jesus says about praying for your enemies in Matthew 5:43–44.

19. Help, Puhleeaze!
Praying for God's Good News to spread

Zach walked out of a Sunday school class on evangelism as baffled as ever. He's tried to tell his friends how to become Christians, but they either pat his head and say "That's nice for you" or just ignore him. "I hate hearing about witnessing and stuff. I know what I'm *supposed* to do," Zach bites, "but I still don't know where to start."

BRAIN DRAIN If you're a Christian, you've grasped the huge news about who God is. What's the best way to start sharing that one-of-a-kind knowledge?

FLASHBACK Maybe you've never thought about the role God wants you to play in his mammoth plan to make friends with the world. Well, God doesn't intend for you to keep him secret. He wants to teach you to speak wisely, to "always be prepared to give an answer to everyone who asks you to give the reason for the hope that you have" (1 Peter 3:15). But whatever you say or do to show people Jesus, you'll do way better if you wrap it in prayer. Even that bit of advice, though, won't help if you don't know what to pray. Here are three chunks to check out. Paul likely wrote two of these—Ephesians and Colossians—while he was shackled to a Roman guard for preaching Christ.

BIBLE CHUNKS Read . . .

Ephesians 6:18–20

> (18) And pray in the Spirit on all occasions with all kinds of prayers and

requests. With this in mind, be alert and always keep on praying for all the saints.

(19) Pray also for me, that whenever I open my mouth, words may be given me so that I will fearlessly make known the mystery of the gospel, (20) for which I am an ambassador in chains. Pray that I may declare it fearlessly, as I should.

Colossians 4:2–6

(2) Devote yourselves to prayer, being watchful and thankful. (3) And pray for us, too, that God may open a door for our message, so that we may proclaim the mystery of Christ, for which I am in chains. (4) Pray that I may proclaim it clearly, as I should. (5) Be wise in the way you act toward outsiders; make the most of every opportunity. (6) Let your conversation be always full of grace, seasoned with salt, so that you may know how to answer everyone.

2 Thessalonians 3:1–2

(1) Finally, brothers, pray for us that the message of the Lord may spread rapidly and be honored, just as it was with you. (2) And pray that we may be delivered from wicked and evil men, for not everyone has faith.

STUFF TO KNOW Squeeze yourself into Paul's shoes as he writes out his "prayer requests." You're a missionary—out to tell the world about Jesus, overseas or at your school. What do you need to survive and succeed?

INSIGHT Roll those passages together and you get lots of things you can pray for yourself—or for others—or for others to pray for you. Spot an example from the Bible Chunks for each of these things-to-ask-God-for:

- Clear words to talk about Christ

- Fearlessness in speaking the message

- Speedy spread of the Good News about Jesus

- Shelter from evil opponents

- Focused, frequent, feisty prayer

- Maturity for God's people

BIG QUESTIONS Those prayer items aren't just for
big-time proclaimers of Christ—like missionaries and moms. Even
Paul—aka "Spiritual Giant of Spiritual Giants"—knew he needed the
boost he'd get through prayer. Yes or no: Would it do you any good
to pray those things for yourself—or to pray with a small group of
friends for God to give all of you all that? How come—or not?

Simple assignment: Think of a friend who's clueless about God.
What would knowing God do for her or him? And is that worth
taking time to pray about?

SIDELIGHT These Bible Chunks don't talk specifically
about praying for non-Christians. In studies 23 and 24 you'll see
how Paul and Jesus prayed for whopper spiritual growth—that
spiritual eyes would be opened and hearts rearranged. That's what
your non-Christian friends need too.

Now that you know what kind of prayer help Paul wanted, got any
ideas of what you could pray about before you try to talk to a friend
or two or twenty about Jesus? What?

SIDELIGHT Telling someone about Jesus without praying
is like throwing yourself up against a refrigerator-sized football
player before you put on pads and a helmet—and get a half-dozen

friends to help. Still, prayer is where you *start*. It isn't where you *stop*. After all, "how can they believe in [Jesus] if they have never heard about him? And how can they hear about him unless someone tells them?" (Romans 10:14 NLT).

DEEP THOT Jesus didn't often utter a specific "Pray for *this*. . . ." But he did say that non-Christians all around you are like a field ripe for harvest—and then commanded, "Pray to the Lord, who owns the harvest, that he will send more workers to gather his harvest" (Matthew 9:38 NCV). Pray for yourself—and for people here, there, and everywhere who are spreading the news about Jesus—to dive into that ripeness and harvest well.

STICKY STUFF Keep Colossians 4:2 in your noggin so you keep on praying for your friends.

PRAY ABOUT IT Pick a friend and pray—both for him or her and for your ability to speak up about Jesus.

DIG ON This one's not a Bible Chunk, but a book. Want to pray for the world? Pick up Patrick Johnstone's *Operation World*, a country-by-country guide to changing your world through prayer.

20. You Talk Too Much
Being quiet with God

By now you've figured out there's a whole lot of ways to pray. Moses talked back to God—with a healthy heap of respect, of course. David—after he'd sinned—kind of crawled back to God on his belly. When Asaph hurt, he wailed. See, prayer is about entering boldly. You can praise, repent, and ask. And yield. But there's one more way to pray. Sometimes it's best to not say a thing.

BRAIN DRAIN What do you think is *not* okay to say to God?

FLASHBACK The book of Job (rhymes with robe, not rob) is toward the middle of the Bible. But history-wise, it tells the story of an early Bible big guy. Job is a well-off man with a nice home and family—until disaster strikes. As Job struggles to understand his suffering, three "friends" try to convince him that his troubles must be God's payback for a hidden evil deed. Job gets mad—so mad that he protests a little too loudly how good he is. This Bible Chunk is the halfway point in a speech where God sets Job straight.

BIBLE CHUNK Read Job 40:1–14

(1) The Lord said to Job:
(2) "Will the one who contends with the Almighty correct him?
Let him who accuses God answer him!"
(3) Then Job answered the Lord:
(4) "I am unworthy—how can I reply to you?
I put my hand over my mouth.

(5) "I spoke once, but I have no answer—
twice, but I will say no more."
(6) Then the Lord spoke to Job out of the storm:
(7) "Brace yourself like a man;
I will question you,
and you shall answer me.
(8) "Would you discredit my justice?
Would you condemn me to justify yourself?
(9) "Do you have an arm like God's,
and can your voice thunder like his?
(10) "Then adorn yourself with glory and splendor,
and clothe yourself in honor and majesty.
(11) "Unleash the fury of your wrath,
look at every proud man and bring him low,
(12) "look at every proud man and humble him,
crush the wicked where they stand.
(13) "Bury them all in the dust together;
shroud their faces in the grave.
(14) "Then I myself will admit to you
that your own right hand can save you."

STUFF TO KNOW At the front end of this chunk,
what does God invite Job to do (verses 1–2)?

INSIGHT A little while back God had asked, "Who is this
that questions my wisdom with such ignorant words?" (Job 38:2
NLT). This chunk makes it clear Job "corrects" God and doubts his
justice—and slams God to make himself look good (verses 2, 8).
God challenges Job to prove his views—and hints that Job is trying
to put together a puzzle when he doesn't have all the pieces.

Job has already listened to a couple Bible chapters of God's correc-
tion. How is he seeing himself about now (verses 3–4)?

DA'SCOOP When Job says he's "not worthy," a more accurate meaning is "I'm small" or "I'm insignificant." He also mumbles something like "I'll shut up now. Really."

How does God pound home his point? What can God do that Job can't (verses 9–14)?

INSIGHT Back in Job 38:4 God pointed out that Job hadn't been around to help make the world. Now God spotlights another thing Job can't do. He asks whether Job has the brains and brawn to rule the universe. That might sound like a grand slam, but it's not. Coming from the totally powerful, totally loving creator of the universe, it's inviting Job to recognize reality.

BIG QUESTIONS How do you react when someone challenges your bad attitude—someone you know is right?

God's truth silenced Job. Fair or unfair?

INSIGHT The Bible is full of prayers spewed straight at God just at the moment life fell apart. God never tells us to stuff a sock in our pain. But he does squash prayers that *tell him what to do*. God's speech to Job responds to people who go beyond wondering how and when his care will arrive to claiming to know better than he does.

Why does Job fall silent? Does he just lose the argument—or does he learn something?

INSIGHT In the end, Job dies old and happy, getting back even more than he had lost. But until that happens, Job doesn't stop claiming to have answers. He gets humble. And he trusts that God knows what's going on, even though he can't see it.

DEEP THOT It's one thing to pour your heart out in prayer. It's another to pretend you know more than God or to dictate how God has to answer your demands. Sometimes the secret of prayer is to quit pleading and screaming—and to rest in quiet awe. Like Psalm 46:10 says, "Be still, and know that I am God."

STICKY STUFF Mull on Psalm 46:10 in some quiet moments.

PRAY ABOUT IT *God, you are great. Teach me to trust your goodness. Help me be quiet with you sometimes.*

DIG ON See what Psalm 32 says about God being your hiding spot—and about listening to his wisdom.

Talk About It • 4

EMPATHIZE: What's going on in your life?
ENCOURAGE: How are you doing with Jesus?
EQUIP: What one truth will you take home today?

- How do you cope when life hurls stuff at your head? (Study 16)
- Who or what is the biggest worry in your life right now? What would you like to tell God about that? (Study 16)
- How do you make big decisions? What's prayer got to do with it? (Study 17)
- When you ask God for guidance, is he going to rip into you and call you stupid? (Study 17)
- What good will it do you to pray for people in authority? (Study 18)
- So what do you do if you think the big guys and gals you're supposed to pray for are bozos? (Study 18)
- What could you pray about if you wanted to tell a friend about Jesus? (Study 19)
- Are there some things it's *not* okay to say to God? (Study 20)
- What's it mean to stop screaming at God and just be awed by him? (Study 20)

PART 5

GRABBING HOLD OF GOD

21. Must-Do Prayer
Making time to pray

When Marcy didn't show up for the must-do prayer session two weeks before her church's spring break mission trip, her team leader wondered what was up. "What's up? You have to ask?" Marcy protested. "I've got homework, student council, and the yearbook has to be to the printer by next Wednesday. I'm too busy. I can't sit still and pray!"

BRAIN DRAIN What in your life gets in the way of time to pray?

FLASHBACK This Bible Chunk highlights a day in the life of Jesus. Well, a couple days. He starts off teaching in the synagogue—a local center of Jewish worship and teaching. He tosses out a demon, kindly heals the mother-in-law of one of his followers, and then—while he's at it—blows away a bunch more demons and heals a bunch more people. And you've gotta see what he does next. . . .

BIBLE CHUNK Read Mark 1:21–39

(21) They went to Capernaum, and when the Sabbath came, Jesus went into the synagogue and began to teach. (22) The people were amazed at his teaching, because he taught them as one who had authority, not as the teachers of the law. (23) Just then a man in their synagogue who was possessed by an evil spirit cried out, (24) "What do you want with us, Jesus of Nazareth? Have you come to destroy us? I know who you are—the Holy One of God!"

(25) "Be quiet!" said Jesus sternly. "Come out of him!" (26) The evil spirit shook the man violently and came out of him with a shriek.

(27) The people were all so amazed that they asked each other, "What is this? A new teaching—and with authority! He even gives orders to evil spirits and they obey him." (28) News about him spread quickly over the whole region of Galilee.

(29) As soon as they left the synagogue, they went with James and John to the home of Simon and Andrew. (30) Simon's mother-in-law was in bed with a fever, and they told Jesus about her. (31) So he went to her, took her hand and helped her up. The fever left her and she began to wait on them.

(32) That evening after sunset the people brought to Jesus all the sick and demon-possessed. (33) The whole town gathered at the door, (34) and Jesus healed many who had various diseases. He also drove out many demons, but he would not let the demons speak because they knew who he was.

(35) Very early in the morning, while it was still dark, Jesus got up, left the house and went off to a solitary place, where he prayed. (36) Simon and his companions went to look for him, (37) and when they found him, they exclaimed: "Everyone is looking for you!"

(38) Jesus replied, "Let us go somewhere else—to the nearby villages—so I can preach there also. That is why I have come." (39) So he traveled throughout Galilee, preaching in their synagogues and driving out demons.

STUFF TO KNOW Jesus preaches. The crowd is wowed. Why (verses 21–22)?

INSIGHT The word for "amazed" here is whomping strong—like getting smacked upside the head. People are astonished because Jesus doesn't have to quote other authorities to support what he says, as did the religious scholars (the "teachers of the law").

Something strange happens as Jesus teaches. What? How's that little interruption turn out (verses 23–26)?

INSIGHT Funny thing: The "evil spirit" spoke truth. Jesus did come to destroy the power of the devil (1 John 3:8), including the devil's horde of "demons," the kind of evil supernatural spirit you see here. Most Bible buffs think Jesus silences the demon so he can show and tell people in his own time who he is. He wants to be known as more than the guy who makes demons shriek.

The people praised Jesus' preaching. How do the people react to his demon-tossing (verses 27–28)?

INSIGHT People are wowed once again. But this time their amazement is tinged with alarm. They'd never seen anything like this. Pretend you're one of Jesus' followers. You're writing a letter home entitled "What I Did Today With Jesus." So what else happens that day (verses 29–34)?

INSIGHT Verses 29–34 and many other places in the Gospels—the Bible books of Matthew, Mark, Luke, and John—show that the healings and demon-tossings that day weren't one-of-a-kind events. Jesus healed *many* and drove out *many* demons.

Now, here's the big point buried in this astounding Bible Chunk. Jesus catches some zzzzzs. And what's he do then (verse 35)?

DA'SCOOP The phrase "very early" literally means "very much at night." Jesus was starting his big-time preaching job. Jesus seeks the strength that only spending time talking with his Father can provide.

BIG QUESTIONS Your job is more about making grades than doing miracles, though some days they're sort of the same thing. But how could making time to pray help your days?

What does prayer have to do with your "ministry," whatever that is—volunteering at school, stuff you do through church, or just helping whoever needs it?

DEEP THOT You think you're too busy to pray? Look at Jesus' day and ponder this: Just when you think there's no time to pray, that's when you need prayer the most. And flip to the next study to see all the reasons early Christians got together to talk to God.

STICKY STUFF You can pray anytime. But in Mark 1:35 Jesus shows you how to start when your day is stuffed.

PRAY ABOUT IT *God, I know what prayer can do. Show me how to make it a priority.*

DIG ON Check out what Luke 5:16, 6:12, and 9:18 say about Jesus getting away to pray.

22. Sweaty-Handed Prayer
Praying with friends

When Brad's hands sweated like a glass of Coke on a hot summer day, Renee thought group prayer seemed way less spiritual than it was supposed to be. When Britney wiped her nose and then twined her fingers with Renee's, Renee wondered who thunk up the rule that you had to hold hands. But when Renee prayed alone, she missed the feeling of closeness to God she got in a group—and how hard everyone worked together to make prayer matter.

BRAIN DRAIN Whazzup about praying with other people? Good idea? Bad idea?

FLASHBACK Having Christian friends isn't an optional good idea. It's about surviving and thriving in your faith. Second Timothy 2:22 tells you what Christian friends can do for you: Together with them you can "flee the evil desires of youth, and pursue righteousness, faith, love and peace, along with those who call on the Lord out of a pure heart." Having someone to "call on the Lord" with is what praying with others is all about.

BIBLE CHUNK Read Matthew 18:19–20

(19) "Again, I tell you that if two of you on earth agree about anything you ask for, it will be done for you by my Father in heaven. (20) For where two or three come together in my name, there am I with them."

STUFF TO KNOW What exactly will happen if two

or three of us earthlings "agree about anything you ask for"? Could
Jesus really mean *whatever* you want (verse 19)?

INSIGHT Who's not into that promise? Round up a friend
or two and agree to pray for a Maserati sports car—or two or
three—and then wait for them to drop from heaven. But before
you make that single verse your life motto, remember this Bible-
reading principle: Get hold of the Bible's *whole* teaching on a subject
to grasp what it says. If you recall 1 John 5:14 ("We can be confident
that he will listen to us whenever we ask him for anything in line
with his will" NLT) you know that this group-prayer promise still
means you and your dudes or dudettes need to ask within God's
will.

So what good does praying together do (verse 19)?

SIDELIGHT Jesus promises a one-of-a-kind experience of
his presence when you link up in prayer—maybe just what you
need to nail down what God wants to give you. He's evidently
really happy to hear people teaming up to pray. And if you want to
know what group prayer can look like, check these examples from
the early church:

- *They prayed together, ummm . . . a lot* (Acts 1:14):
  They all joined together constantly in prayer, along with the
  women and Mary the mother of Jesus, and with his brothers.
- *The prayed together because it was a priority* (Acts 2:42):
  They devoted themselves to the apostles' teaching and to the
  fellowship, to the breaking of bread and to prayer.
- *They prayed together for guidance* (Acts 1:24–25):
  Then they prayed, "Lord, you know everyone's heart. Show us

which of these two you have chosen to take over this apostolic ministry."

- *They prayed together for more of God* (Acts 4:24, 31):
  They raised their voices together in prayer to God. "Sovereign Lord," they said, "you made the heaven and the earth and the sea, and everything in them. . . ." After they prayed, the place where they were meeting was shaken. And they were all filled with the Holy Spirit and spoke the word of God boldly.

- *They prayed together at the beach* (Acts 21:5):
  But when our time was up, we left and continued on our way. All the disciples and their wives and children accompanied us out of the city, and there on the beach we knelt to pray.

- *They prayed together in prison* (Acts 16:25):
  About midnight Paul and Silas were praying and singing hymns to God, and the other prisoners were listening to them.

- *They prayed together for persecuted believers* (Acts 12:5):
  So Peter was kept in prison, but the church was earnestly praying to God for him.

- *They prayed together when they faced a crisis—like a shipwreck* (Acts 27:29):
  Fearing that we would be dashed against the rocks, they dropped four anchors from the stern and prayed for daylight.

- *They prayed together to launch people into ministry* (Acts 13:3):
  So after they had fasted and prayed, they placed their hands on them and sent them off.

From what you see in all those brief Bible Chunks, why was praying together important to early Christians?

BIG QUESTIONS Does praying with people make talking to God easier or harder for you?

What do you gain from talking together with God—stuff you wouldn't get otherwise?

So who *wouldn't* you be deathly afraid to pray with? What would it be cool to pray about together?

DEEP THOT Your relationship with Jesus might feel so private that you'd sooner have your underwear run up a flagpole than be part of praying with others. But remember: Praying together is a privilege—and a cool experience unlike any other. And there's no rule in the Bible that says you have to hold hands.

STICKY STUFF Put Matthew 18:19–20 in your head. And put your head together with someone else.

PRAY ABOUT IT Grab a friend and talk to God.

DIG ON Check out the passages surrounding any of those group prayer Bible Chunks—to see how prayer fits in the whole story.

(23.) Insanely Huge Explosive Power

Praying to know God better

Way back in this book you read that when your prayer is to get close to God and live according to his will, God's answers are mind-blowing: "By his mighty power at work within us," the Bible promises, "he is able to accomplish infinitely more than we would ever dare to ask or hope" (Ephesians 3:20 NLT). Well, in the next two studies you get two of the greatest prayers of the New Testament— a two-pronged approach to huge spiritual growth that points you closer to God and his people.

BRAIN DRAIN You've made it this far in *Pray Hard*, so it's clear you want to grow spiritually. How close can you get to God? How spiritually mature can you get?

FLASHBACK The people in the city of Ephesus were no strangers to Paul. He lived with and taught the Christians there for two years (Acts 19:1–10). They became wise friends who saved him when a mob of thousands wanted to rip him to pieces for bad-mouthing their mega-goddess Artemis (Acts 19:23–41). Paul and the Ephesians cried and prayed together when Paul sailed away to almost-certain imprisonment and death (Acts 20:36–37). When Paul writes them from prison, he's not correcting a whole lot. He's writing to tell them how huge they can grow.

BIBLE CHUNK Read Ephesians 1:15–20; 3:16–19

(1:15) For this reason, ever since I heard about your faith in the Lord Jesus and your love for all the saints, (1:16) I have not stopped giving thanks for you, remembering you in my prayers. (1:17) I keep asking that the God of our Lord Jesus Christ, the glorious Father, may give you the Spirit of wisdom and revelation, so that you may know him better. (1:18) I pray also that the eyes of your heart may be enlightened in order that you may know the hope to which he has called you, the riches of his glorious inheritance in the saints, (1:19) and his incomparably great power for us who believe. That power is like the working of his mighty strength, (1:20) which he exerted in Christ when he raised him from the dead. . . .

(3:16) I pray that out of his glorious riches he may strengthen you with power through his Spirit in your inner being, (3:17) so that Christ may dwell in your hearts through faith. And I pray that you, being rooted and established in love, (3:18) may have power, together with all the saints, to grasp how wide and long and high and deep is the love of Christ, (3:19) and to know this love that surpasses knowledge—that you may be filled to the measure of all the fullness of God.

STUFF TO KNOW What great spiritual traits have the Ephesians already got (verse 1:15)?

What more does Paul ask God to give them? Why (verse 1:17)?

INSIGHT Jesus said that when he returned to heaven the Holy Spirit would come and "teach you all things and will remind you of everything I have said to you" (John 14:26). That same Holy Spirit gives "revelation" or insight into Christ. And to "know him better" means you get firsthand knowledge, not regurgitated facts about God wiped up from someone else.

What other whopper stuff does Paul pray for? And what triple-good thing will that accomplish (verses 1:18–19)?

DA'SCOOP "Hope" means the present and future good times you'll have because you know God—here and in heaven. The rich "inheritance in the saints" is either one of two things: It's the friendship we get with God or the friendship he gets with us. And the phrases "incomparably great power for us who believe" and "working of his mighty strength" string together words that mean God works in us with an insanely huge explosive power that's under perfect control, like a bazillion nuclear power plants with no chance of breakdown. It's the same power that blasted Christ clear out of the grave.

So where's all that power wind up (verse 3:16)?

And what'll that do fer ya (verses 3:17–19)?

INSIGHT Here's the result of that heap of stuff: You'll know God in a way you never imagined. You'll be absolutely stuffed full of his love.

Easy guess: Do you think this is a prayer Paul uttered once for the folks at Ephesus—and then forgot (verse 1:16)?

BIG QUESTIONS Would you believe it if someone said the start into this mind-blowing experience of God is simply *asking* him for it? What do you want to do with that offer?

Paul probably prayed those kinds of prayers for himself, and you can do that. But who in your life could agree to pray that prayer for you?

One last question to mull. Name one or two non-Christians you know who could stand to have "the eyes of their heart" enlightened about Jesus. Will you plaster their names somewhere to remind you to pray for them?

DEEP THOT Rare is the offer to give you even more than you ask for. Dream big—and you'll get even more of God.

STICKY STUFF You can't do better than to pray Ephesians 1:17.

PRAY ABOUT IT *God, give me your Holy Spirit of wisdom and revelation so I can know you better. Open the eyes of my heart so I can grasp how wide and long and high and deep is the love of Christ.*

DIG ON Read about Paul's relationship with his Ephesian friends in Acts 19.

24. Jesus' Almost-Last Request
Praying to know God's people better

Michael sneers at his youth pastor across the lunch table. Yeah, all the youth from church had agreed to sit together once a week when he visited school. Now Michael has two things to gag about—hot lunch *and* several people he didn't want to be seen with. But when one of the cutest and coolest girls in school walks up and says getting together is a good idea, he starts to think this isn't so dumb. . . .

BRAIN DRAIN What good does it do you to hang out with other Christians—besides catching babes or boys?

FLASHBACK Matthew, Mark, and Luke tell us that right before his arrest and crucifixion, Jesus went to the Garden of Gethsemane to pray—that's the prayer you read where Jesus struggles with his Father's will. John records an event just prior to that—this time where Jesus prays about his own relationship with his Father, the relationship he wants his followers to have with God, and the relationship he plans for us to have with one another. If you're looking for ways to pray for big spiritual growth, scoop this. They're words important enough to be Jesus' almost-last request.

BIBLE CHUNK Read John 17:1-5, 11, 13-23

(1) After Jesus said this, he looked toward heaven and prayed:
"Father, the time has come. Glorify your Son, that your Son may

glorify you. (2) For you granted him authority over all people that he might give eternal life to all those you have given him. (3) Now this is eternal life: that they may know you, the only true God, and Jesus Christ, whom you have sent. (4) I have brought you glory on earth by completing the work you gave me to do. (5) And now, Father, glorify me in your presence with the glory I had with you before the world began. . . .

(11) "I will remain in the world no longer, but they are still in the world, and I am coming to you. Holy Father, protect them by the power of your name—the name you gave me—so that they may be one as we are one. . . .

(13) "I am coming to you now, but I say these things while I am still in the world, so that they may have the full measure of my joy within them. (14) I have given them your word and the world has hated them, for they are not of the world any more than I am of the world. (15) My prayer is not that you take them out of the world but that you protect them from the evil one. (16) They are not of the world, even as I am not of it. (17) Sanctify them by the truth; your word is truth. (18) As you sent me into the world, I have sent them into the world. (19) For them I sanctify myself, that they too may be truly sanctified.

(20) "My prayer is not for them alone. I pray also for those who will believe in me through their message, (21) that all of them may be one, Father, just as you are in me and I am in you. May they also be in us so that the world may believe that you have sent me. (22) I have given them the glory that you gave me, that they may be one as we are one: (23) I in them and you in me. May they be brought to complete unity to let the world know that you sent me and have loved them even as you have loved me."

STUFF TO KNOW Jesus wants his Father in heaven to do something for him. What? How come (verses 1, 5)?

INSIGHT Hard as it is for us to grasp, Jesus and the Father are both fully God—and, along with the Holy Spirit, they're a "Trinity," three "persons" in one "being," as Bible buffs explain. When Jesus came to walk on planet earth he shed his heavenly splendor. He asks the Father to give him that back.

Loads of people think eternal life is just living for a *reeeeeallly* long time. How does Jesus define it (verse 3)?

Jesus knows he's headed for the cross—and, on the other side of that, back to heaven. What does he want his all-powerful Father to do for his followers (verse 11)?

If the Father does that, what will happen (peek at the very end of verse 11)?

INSIGHT The world isn't happy with Jesus' followers (verse 14) because they lack the world's hostility to God. So it's a good thing we can get near God and his protection (verses 11, 15). When Jesus says he and the Father are "one," they're as close as they can get without losing their identities. It's that three-in-one "Trinity" thing.

What does Jesus ask for *us*—the people "who believe in me through their message" (verses 20–21)?

And what will happen if that happens (two things—one in verse 21, one in verse 23)?

BIG QUESTIONS How could sticking tight with other Christians help you when the world thinks you're not so hot?

Isn't love *just supposed to happen*? Or wait a second—isn't loving someone your *choice*? Why pray for getting close to other Christians?

If what Jesus says is true, what can happen if people see you and your friends caring for each other?

DEEP THOT You maybe know that God's two greatest commandments are to "love the Lord your God with all your heart and with all your soul and with all your mind" and to "love your neighbor as yourself" (Matthew 22:37, 39). These last couple Bible Chunks show you how to ask God to do that stuff in you.

STICKY STUFF Shoot John 17:23 up a snotty nose.

PRAY ABOUT IT *God, make me and my friends one—so everyone will know Jesus is God and loves us beyond belief.*

DIG ON Check out a cool passage on getting along with your Christian brothers and sisters in 1 John 4:7–21.

25. Can You Trust This Guy?
Believing God is good

Leaning over the rail sounds like a good idea—until the boat lurches on a wave and punches into your stomach like a waist-wide Heimlich maneuver. Everything you've eaten in the last month feels like it's an inch from becoming fish bait, and your uncle just laughs. You wish he'd turn back for shore as the boat keeps rocking . . . rolling . . . heaving . . . dropping. But he just keeps casting for fish with a hearty chuckle. You're wondering why your parents trusted you out in a boat with this guy. And you sure wish he'd stop singing *Yo, ho, ho. . . .*

BRAIN DRAIN You're going through life and suddenly you're slammed by a storm that will sink you—or at least make you sick. You know you *can* pray to God. But do you trust him enough to *want* to pray to him?

FLASHBACK This Bible Chunk takes place on the Sea of Galilee—a lake, actually, surrounded by steep mountains with narrow valleys. When winds whip down toward the lake, sudden, strong storms break out—storms big enough to scare a bunch of fishermen.

BIBLE CHUNK Read Luke 8:22–25

(22) One day Jesus said to his disciples, "Let's go over to the other side of the lake." So they got into a boat and set out. (23) As they sailed, he fell asleep. A squall came down on the lake, so that the boat was being

swamped, and they were in great danger.

(24) The disciples went and woke him, saying, "Master, Master, we're going to drown!"

He got up and rebuked the wind and the raging waters; the storm subsided, and all was calm. (25) "Where is your faith?" he asked his disciples.

In fear and amazement they asked one another, "Who is this? He commands even the winds and the water, and they obey him."

STUFF TO KNOW Jesus had told his dozen closest

followers they should go to the other side of the lake. So they get in a boat and go. How's Jesus feeling about getting bounced by that storm (verse 23)?

Several of Jesus' followers were fishermen. How can they be so afraid (verses 23–24)?

INSIGHT Luke three times mentions the wind, as if to em-

phasize the severity of the squall (verses 23–25). Those fisher guys knew the water. They knew the weather. What they didn't know so well was their master's power.

So the disciples wake Jesus. Does it sound like they're expecting him to save them? Or do they just want him to put on a life jacket (verse 24)?

SIDELIGHT So far in the Bible book of Luke Jesus' follow-

ers have seen him cast out demons and heal physical afflictions (4:31–41). He'd healed a man who couldn't walk (5:17–26) and even raised a widow's son from the dead (7:11–16). But so far Jesus hasn't applied his power to nature—to something nonliving. Given their reaction to the miracle he's about to do, it looks like they just wanted him to bail water.

What does Jesus do? How? Are you impressed (verse 24)?

You'd think the guys would say, "Jesus, we just knew you could do it!" But how do they react (verse 25)?

And what's Jesus' big question for them (verse 25)?

INSIGHT When Jesus says, "Where is your faith?" he's saying, "You don't get who I am." And they don't. Out pops this question from the disciples: "Who is this?"

BIG QUESTIONS You've already said whether you're quick to pray in the storms of life. When those life storms hit, are you confused about who God is and his ability to help you—like the disciples?

If you said no, that's great. But if you said yes, you're normal. What do you suppose convinced the disciples that Jesus was worth trusting?

INSIGHT Here's the truth: It's hard to pray if you don't trust God deep down. But even Jesus' biggest followers took a long time to learn who he was. It also took them until after his death for them to learn to pray. Jesus notices their lack of faith in the boat, but he doesn't mock them for it. He calmly meets their need. And kindly saves them from a fatal swim.

So what are you going to do to keep learning to trust and to pray?

DEEP THOT Jesus opened the way for you to talk to God. When you understand that God is worth trusting, you'll talk to him with total confidence.

STICKY STUFF Tuck Luke 8:24–25 in your brain before you get tossed over the side.

PRAY ABOUT IT *God, help me to trust you more and more each day. And help that trust to make it easier for me to pray.*

DIG ON Read Matthew 11:28–30 for a reminder of why you run to God.

Talk About It • 5

EMPATHIZE: What's going on in your life?
ENCOURAGE: How are you doing with Jesus?
EQUIP: What one truth will you take home today?

- What in your life gets in the way of time to pray? (Study 21)
- Your job probably is more about making grades than making miracles. So how does making time to pray help your days? (Study 21)
- Whazzup about praying with other people? Good idea? Bad idea? (Study 22)
- Does praying with people make talking to God easier or harder for you? (Study 22)
- How close can you get to God? Who in your life will pray for you to get closer? (Study 23)
- How could sticking tight with other Christians help you when the world thinks you're not so hot? (Study 24)
- If all the stuff Jesus prayed in John 17 is true, what can happen if people see you and your friends caring for each other? (Study 24)
- By now you know you *can* pray to God. You know *what* to pray about. But do you *want* to pray to him? (Study 25)
- Do you think that God is the guy to turn to when life gets stormy? (Study 25)

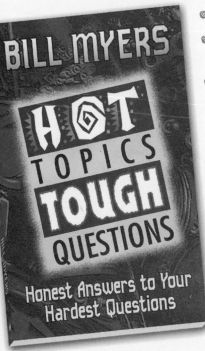

THANKS FOR PICKING A BETHANY BOOK

Bethany House Publishers is part of Bethany Fellowship
International, a group of Christians who want to reach the
world with God's Good News about Jesus by starting churches,
printing Christian books, and caring for the poor. Bethany
College of Missions is a school that trains missionaries.

If you would like to know more about what we do, please write:

Bethany Fellowship International
6820 Auto Club Road
Minneapolis, MN 55438 USA